Baedeker Jerusalem

...ton
Hotel

Ocean   Fish

Med Eastern   KING DAVID
               Mid orit

Baedeker's

JERUSALEM

Imprint

Cover picture: Dome of the Rock and the Western (Wailing) Wall

99 colour photographs
12 plans, 1 drawing, 1 large city map

Conception and editorial work:
Redaktionsbüro Harenberg, Schwerte
English language: Alec Court

Text:
Bernhard Pollmann; revision and additional material Baedeker Editorial Department

General direction:
Dr Peter Baumgarten, Baedeker Stuttgart

English translation: Babel Translations Norwich

Cartography:
Ingenieurbüro für Kartographie Huber & Oberländer, Munich
Carta, Jerusalem (city map)

Source of illustrations:
Bilderdienst Suddeutscher Verlag (1), Preussischer Kulturbesitz (2), Rogge (27),
Sperber (69)

Following the tradition established by Karl Baedeker in 1844, sights of particular interest and hotels of outstanding quality are distinguished by either one or two asterisks.

To make it easier to locate the various sights listed in the "A to Z" section of the Guide, their coordinates on the large map of central Jerusalem are shown in red at the head of each entry.

Only a selection of hotels, shops and restaurants can be given: no reflection is implied, therefore, on establishments not included.

In a time of rapid change it is difficult to ensure that all the information given is entirely accurate and up to date, and the possibility of error can never be entirely eliminated. Although the publishers can accept no responsibility for inaccuracies and omissions they are always grateful for corrections and suggestions for improvement.

Contents

Preface

This Pocket Guide to Jerusalem is one of the new generation of Baedeker city guides.

Baedeker pocket guides, illustrated throughout in colour, are designed to meet the needs of the modern traveller. They are quick and easy to consult, with the principal sights described in alphabetical order and practical details about opening times, how to get there, etc., shown in the margin.

Each guide is divided into three parts. The first part gives a general account of the city, its history, population, culture and so on; in the second part the principal sights are described; and the third part contains a variety of practical information designed to help visitors to find their way about and make the most of their stay.

The new guides are abundantly illustrated and contain numbers of newly drawn plans. At the back of the book is a large city map, and each entry in the main part of the guide gives the coordinates of the square on the map in which the particular feature can be located. Users of this guide, therefore, will have no difficulty in finding what they want to see.

Facts and Figures

Arms of the
City of Jerusalem

General

The State of Israel was founded on 14 May 1948 as a parliamentary republic. Its supreme legislature is its Parliament, the Knesset, which has 120 members. The representative head of state is the President (since March 1983, Chaim Herzog), who is elected for a five-year term and may only stand for one further term of office. The President is responsible for nominating the Prime Minister (1977–83 Menachem Begin) who is elected by the Knesset to head the Government.
Israel does not have a written Constitution. In 1950 the Knesset decided to introduce a number of constitutional laws that would later serve as the basis for a Constitution since there was failure to agree on just how much scope should be allowed for the religious laws. An absolute majority in the Knesset is required to pass any constitutional law. A constitutional law on human rights is currently in the course of preparation.

From the Declaration of Independence:
"The State of Israel shall be open to Jewish immigration and In-gathering of the Exiles; it shall dedicate the development of the country to the prosperity of all its people; it shall be founded on freedom, justice and peace in the spirit of the vision of the Prophets of Israel; it shall guarantee all its citizens equal social and political rights without distinction as to race, sex or creed; it shall vouchsafe them freedom of thought and of conscience, and freedom of culture and speech; it shall continue to stay true to the principles of the United Nations Charter."

The official languages are modern Hebrew (Ivrit, a modern version of the language of the Old Testament) and Arabic. English is the unofficial language of commerce.

In 1950 West Jerusalem was declared capital of Israel instead of Tel Aviv. Most states have not recognised this decision. In 1947 the United Nations had proposed international status for Jerusalem. During the Six Day War in 1967 Israel occupied East Jerusalem, the Arab sector of the city that had belonged to Jordan, and united it, in administrative terms, with Israeli West Jerusalem.
On 29 July 1980 the UN General Assembly called on Israel to withdraw from all the occupied territories, including East Jerusalem. On 30 July 1980 the Israeli Parliament declared the whole city of Jerusalem to be the capital of Israel. Prime Minister Begin wished to transfer the government quarter from West to East Jerusalem.

Jerusalem is in eastern Israel in the Judean Hills on the edge of the desert, about 38 miles/60 km E of the Mediterranean and about 18 miles/30 km W of the Dead Sea on 35° longitude E and 32° latitude N.

State

Official languages

De facto capital

Situation

◀ *Symbols of Jerusalem: the Western (Wailing) Wall and Dome of the Rock*

General

Area and population

Israeli West Jerusalem covers 15 sq. miles/38 sq. km. If one includes East Jerusalem, occupied since 1967, the whole city of Jerusalem covers an area of 42 sq. miles/108 sq. km. The plan is to create an administrative area of Greater Jerusalem.
In 1984 Jerusalem as a whole had a population of 430,000, of which 315,000 were Jews. In 1980 there were 99,066 Palestinian refugees living in the Jerusalem area, 17,775 of them in camps (see Population).

Administration

Jerusalem's mayor and 33 city councillors are directly elected by all the people of Jerusalem entitled to vote. The City Administration's departments are headed by four deputy mayors. One deputy mayor is the Mayor's permanent representative.

Districts

Jerusalem has about 150 districts and separate residential quarters.
The Old Town within the walls is the historic heart of the city. It is divided into Armenian, Jewish, Arab and Christian quarters. Because of overpopulation the Christian quarter cannot accept any more new residents. The Armenian quarter is a walled enclave within the Old Town (see A–Z, Armenian Quarter). The Jewish quarter has been rebuilt since 1967 and its residents are supposed to be exclusively Jewish (650 families will live there when reconstruction is complete).
Teddy Kollek, Mayor of Jerusalem since 1965, favours the introduction of a system of boroughs, with each quarter of the city responsible for its own administration. These plans also include taking over the Ottoman Millet system. Administrative boundaries will not be determined solely on geographical

Easy-to-read multilingual traffic signs

grounds but ethnic and religious groups will acquire the possibility of relative autonomy in their own districts. In 1981 the city as a whole had five self-administered districts, including an Arab one.

Transport

Within Jerusalem buses and taxis are the main form of transport. The problem of too much heavy vehicle traffic on the streets of Jerusalem, despite planning that favours the motorist without antagonising the pedestrian, is the same as in other big cities. The Old Town is largely closed to vehicles. There are plans to turn a number of streets in West Jerusalem into pedestrian precincts.

Inside the city

Transport outside the city is by buses and taxis using a well-developed road system. There are also rail links with Tel Aviv, Haifa and Beersheba.

Outside the city

Ben Gurion International Airport at Lod, between Jerusalem and Tel Aviv, is served by 20 international airlines. Atarot, N of Jerusalem, caters for domestic flights, mainly to Haifa and Tel Aviv.

Airport

Population and Religion

Jerusalem is the seat of the Knesset, the Supreme Court, the Chief Rabbinate, an Israeli and an Arab district authority and ten Ministries. Since no heavy industry is permitted, 75% of Jerusalem's population is engaged on administration. In 1984 Jerusalem's population totalled 430,000, of whom 315,000 were Jews.

Administration in the city

Jerusalem's main population problems stem from the antagonism between Arabs and Jews, as well as between easterners and westerners. The birthrate has a large part to play in this. Jerusalem has the highest birth figures in the country. 16% of the families have seven or more children, 39% of the population is of school age.
The families with the high birthrates are mostly Arab or eastern Jews. Because of this high birthrate and, at the same time, a fall in Jewish immigration from Western countries, there are many who fear that Jerusalem could become an Arab city by nature, and certainly have more eastern influence.

Population problems

Jerusalem, in Hebrew Yerushalayim ("city of peace"), in Arabic El-Quds ("the shrine"), is the Holy City of three of the world's religions.
The Jews have the oldest established rights to Jerusalem since in 1004 B.C. King David raised Jerusalem to the status of the capital of the United Kingdom of the Israelites. The holiest place for the Jews is the Wailing Wall, a western section of the wall that once surrounded the temple precinct.
The importance for Christians of Jerusalem is that it was the scene of the final incidents in the life of Christ. Here he was judged, executed and entombed. The holiest place in

Holy City

A diversity of peoples and religions

Jerusalem for Christians is the Church of the Holy Sepulchre.
For Moslems Jerusalem is the third holiest city after Mecca and
Medina since they believe that it was from Haram esh-Sharif,
the rock of the Temple Mount, that Mohammed ascended into
heaven. The Moslems' holiest sites in Jerusalem are the El Aqsa
Mosque and the Dome of the Rock in Haram esh-Sharif.

The population trend in terms of religious affiliation:

	1844	1896	1948	1967	1977
Jews	7,120	28,112	100,000	195,700	265,000
Moslems	5,000	8,560	40,000	54,960	89,300
Christians	3,390	8,748	25,000	10,800	12,000
Total	15,510	45,420	165,000	261,460	366,300

(Source: "Profile of Israel", published by the Israeli Information
Centre, Jerusalem.)

These figures do not show the breakdown into the individual
religious communities. There are 34 different Christian
denominations in Jerusalem alone. The most important are the
Greek Orthodox, the Roman Catholics and the Armenians. For
the relationships between the Christian sects, see A–Z, Church
of the Holy Sepulchre.
The majority of Jerusalem's Arabs are Sunnite Moslems. There
are also many Christian Arabs.
The main distinction among the Jews is between the Ashkenazi
and the Sephardi. The Ashkenazi are Jews and their
descendants who came from Central and Eastern Europe. They
have their own traditions and their own language, Yiddish. The
Sephardi are Jews from Spain and Portugal who also have their
own language (Ladino) and traditions. The supreme judicial
authority for the Jews on religious matters is the Chief
Rabbinate, consisting of an Ashkenazi and a Sephardi Chief
Rabbi, and the Supreme Rabbinical Council.
The Jews in the Me'a She'arim quarter form a special group.
They do not recognise the State of Israel because it did not
adopt the Torah, the laws of Moses, as its Constitution. They
pay no taxes and have had their own currency for some time.
These strictly Orthodox Jews still dress as they did in the
eastern European ghettos of 300 years ago. Every aspect of
their lives is governed by the Torah. In this quarter time appears
to have stood still for centuries.

Culture

Thanks to Teddy Kollek (see Famous People), Jerusalem has
become Israel's cultural centre. Besides its two universities,
with about 20,000 students, special mention should be made
of the Academy of Sciences, innumerable scientific institutes
and research centres, medical colleges, museums, libraries,
theatres, sports centres, etc. In addition Jerusalem is also the
headquarters of Kol Israel, the Voice of Israel, the national
broadcasting corporation, and Israeli television. The regional
and national newspapers are published in Jerusalem and a
number of publishing and printing houses have their head
offices here.

Students of the Torah deep in discussion

The Torah: the fundamental law of the Jews

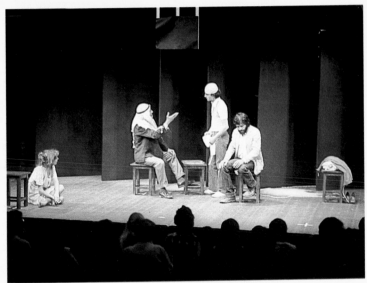

Jerusalem as a cultural centre: performance at the Khan Theatre

Commerce and Industry

Heavy industry is not permitted in Jerusalem; only 17% of its people work in industry, most of which is based on traditional occupations such as diamond cutting, glass-making, the manufacture of shoes and leather goods, the electrical and pharmaceutical industries, etc. Cigarette-making is also of importance. A large proportion of the jobs are in printing and publishing.

The main source of income in East Jerusalem – which includes the Old Town – is tourism. The bulk of the visitors are pilgrims.

Famous People

After the death of the first king of the Israelites, Saul, who had been repudiated by the Hebrew God, Yahweh (or Jehovah), David was anointed king of Judah in Hebron and was later recognised as ruler of the 12 tribes of the United Kingdom. The books of Samuel in the Old Testament recount the legends and stories surrounding the rise of David, the shepherd boy from

David
(reign: 1004–965 B.C.)

Bethlehem, his first anointing as "the chosen one of Yahweh", his time as a page and harpist at the court of Saul, his fight with Goliath, the mighty champion of the Philistines, and his enmity with Saul, whom David, once he became successful, soon came to see only as a hated rival. The continual tension between Israel in the N and Judah in the S hastened the choice of a neutral seat of power: David seized the city of the Jebusites (Jerusalem) which until then had remained aloof. The Jebusites who lived there were allowed to remain and supported the new king. Jerusalem was enlarged to form the capital and had a wall built around it. The acropolis, called Zion by the Jebusites, became known as the City of David.

The construction and fortification of the capital followed the lodging there of the Ark of the Covenant (symbol of Yahweh's presence). Thus David made Jerusalem the political and intellectual centre of a kingdom that stretched from the Mediterranean to the deserts of Arabia.

To judge from the Old Testament, in his person David embodied the ruler pleasing in the sight of God, both a statesman and a poet, general and musician, singing the praises of Yahweh. All future kings were judged in the light of his kingship. It was true that he was guilty of lapses – such as the dance in front of the Ark of the Covenant when it was brought to Jerusalem – but he never turned away from Yahweh and his greatest sin was forgiven him: when David saw Bath-sheba bathing, the wife of his earlier comrade-in-arms Uriah, he had her summoned to his presence. Bath-sheba became pregnant, whereupon David arranged for Uriah to fight in the front rank in a battle, where he met his death.

David repented of his deed and implored Yahweh's forgiveness. David married Bath-sheba once her mourning period was over and she gave birth to Solomon, his successor (see entry). David wanted to build a temple for the Ark of the Covenant but he was told by the prophets that this task would fall to Solomon. David died at the age of 70 and was buried in Jerusalem, although it is not known exactly where (see A–Z, Mount Zion: David's Tomb).

St Helena
(c. 257–c. 337)

St Helena, the mother of Constantine the Great, was the foundress of nearly all the early Christian church buildings in and around Jerusalem.

Helena, owner of an inn in Bithynia, later became the mistress of the man who was destined to become the emperor Constantius Chlorus. The offspring of their union was Constantine the Great. She was converted to Christianity in 312. This conversion preceded Constantine's religious experiences, which are said to have resulted in the Edicts of Milan (313, the "Tolerance" edict). These reports are, however, shrouded in legend and not very reliable. Before a decisive battle Constantine is said to have seen a vision of a cross with the words "in this sign conquer". His mother, who in 325 had been elevated to the rank of an Augustan, followed her son's request to make a pilgrimage to Jerusalem and there sought – and found – the True Cross (see A–Z, Church of the Holy Sepulchre: Chapel of Helena and Crypt of the Finding of the Cross).

Helena's discoveries in the Holy Land – mainly in the form of holy relics – resulted in a great many church buildings of which the most worthy of mention are the churches of the Holy Sepulchre in Jerusalem and of the Nativity in Bethlehem. The relics of the Cross were taken to Rome where they are put on display every year on Good Friday and on 3 May in the Church of Santa Croce in Gerusalemme.

Helena died at the age of 80, probably in Rome, where she was first interred close by the Via Labicana. Constantine had her body taken to Constantinople. Her sarcophagus can today be seen in the Vatican Museum. In the 9th c. St Helena's relics were taken to Hautvilliers Abbey in France. Today they are to be found in the Church of Santa Maria in Aracoeli in Rome.

Herod I – often termed the ruler most obsessed with building in antiquity, and at the same time the most hated and most schismatic of the potentates of Jerusalem, was the only one to be known as "the Great". He was born in 73 B.C. in Idumea, which had been forcibly incorporated into Judah, the son of the royal governor Antipatros and the Arab princess Kypros. After Antipatros was murdered the Roman triumvir Mark Antony appointed him tetrarch in 42 B.C. but during the struggle for the throne of Judah Herod was forced to flee to Rome. There, in 40 B.C., the Senate proclaimed him king of Judah. After Jerusalem had been captured and many of the Jewish nobility had been executed Herod became ruler in 37 B.C.

Herod the Great
(*c.* 73 B.C.–4 B.C.)

Herod's policy was markedly one of forging close links with Rome and constantly attempting to unite the Roman Pax Romana with Hellenism. Under his government Palestine experienced an unrivalled economic boom and more than 30 years of peace. The religious worship of the Jews was, until the eagle was mounted on the Temple shortly before Herod's death, left untouched, but the tendency towards Hellenisation did encounter opposition from the Orthodox Jews. Any opposition was ruthlessly suppressed.

The country's prosperity was also reflected in the high rate of building activity which Herod made possible without an increase in taxes. Besides the construction of the cities of Samaria and Caesarea (the largest port complex in antiquity), his principal interest lay in building up and beautifying Jerusalem. The Antonia Fortress was erected above the Temple Square, in the N arose a quarter with theatre and circus buildings, the three towers of the citadel in the western part of town even outlasted the destruction of Jerusalem by the Romans and the city's water supply was substantially improved. About 20 B.C. Herod was responsible for the converting and rebuilding of the Temple which, in terms of magnificence and dimensions, completely dwarfed the previous complex. Since the destruction of this temple in A.D. 70 the holiest place for the Jews is the "Wailing Wall" (since 1967 officially known as the West Wall) which formed part of the encircling wall on the western side of the Temple.

Other buildings that took shape under Herod's rule included the rock fortress of Massada on the Dead Sea, the luxurious fort of Herodion near Bethlehem, the complex above the Mach-pelah Cave of the patriarchs in Hebron, the winter residence in Jericho, etc.

Christian tradition, literature and, in a grotesque way, also historical writings describe Herod as a bloodthirsty tyrant, the most monstrous man in the world, as a raving mad despot, who wanted to impress the Jews by an excessive show of grandeur and a massive boost to their economy; as the builder of forts to tyrannise the people; as the murderer, mad with jealousy and blind with lust, of his wife, Mariamne; and as the inhuman brute, damned for all eternity, who gave the order for the massacre of the Innocents in Bethlehem (cf. Grotto of the Innocents in the Church of the Nativity, Bethlehem).

Herod died at Jericho "of a repulsive disease which in the history books only strikes down those people who have dishonoured themselves through their cruelty and bloodlust" (Anton P. Chekhov, Russian doctor and poet).

Josephus Flavius, the Jewish historian, describes how Herod's body was taken in a magnificent procession from Jericho to Herodion, near Bethlehem, where Herod had already had his mausoleum built during his lifetime. Although tombs have been discovered in Herodion, Herod's grave has yet to come to light.

Theodor Herzl
(2.5.1860–3.7.1904)

Theodor Herzl is the founder of political Zionism and in essence the establishment of the State of Israel results from the ideas that he formulated.

Born a Jew in Budapest in 1860, he became a Doctor of Philosophy in Vienna in 1884 at a time when anti-semitic outbursts at Vienna University were rife. From 1891 to 1895 he was a foreign correspondent in Paris where the anti-semitic attitude of large sections of the population, particularly during the Dreyfus affair, decided him to take up the cause of Zionism. After returning from Paris Herzl published the Zionist Manifesto, "The Jewish State", in Vienna in 1896. In this he called for a sovereign Jewish state to be established not only on the grounds that the Jews were a religious community but also because they were a nation in their own right. He suggested Argentina and Palestine as possible emigration venues and he saw the constitution of the future Jewish state as a kind of constitutional monarchy or an aristocratic republic.

In 1897 Herzl summoned the first Zionist Congress. This met in Basle where the Zionist movement made its official platform the fact that "Zionism seeks to obtain for the Jewish people a publicly recognised, legally secured homeland in Palestine". An entry in Herzl's diary for 3.9.1897 reads, "At Basle I founded the Jewish State. In five years perhaps, and certainly in fifty years, everyone will perceive it." (Cf. also Quotations.)

The negotiations for the establishment of a Jewish State conducted by Herzl as President of the World Zionist Organisation, with the Sultan and several European rulers, including Wilhelm II and the Pope, came to nothing.

After Israel was founded the body of the Zionist leader was brought from Vienna to Mount Herzl in Jerusalem (see A–Z, Mount Herzl). Here every year the opening ceremony of Israel's Independence Day takes place. At the entrance to the park around his tomb is the Herzl Museum, in which one of the exhibits is his study, also brought here from Vienna, in which he wrote his book "Old–New Land".

Teddy Kollek
(b. 27.5.1911)

The Mayor of Jerusalem since 1965, Teddy Kollek was born in Nagyvaszony, near Budapest, in 1911, the son of a Jewish official. He joined in the youth movement of the Zionist Socialists, took part in the Congresses after 1923 and, in 1930, entered an agricultural training centre for the settlement by the Jews of Palestine. In 1935 he emigrated to Palestine and founded the En Gev Kibbutz on the eastern shore of the Sea of Galilee.

After various missions for the Zionist movement, including

undercover work in Istanbul in the Second World War, Kollek was in New York from 1947 laying the foundations for the establishment of the State of Israel by arms deals, smuggling and, above all, collecting funds from American Jews. From 1952 to 1964 he headed the Prime Minister's office of the new state and after his resignation in 1965 obtained the candidature for the office of Mayor of Jerusalem.

Today Jerusalem is the city of Teddy Kollek. No other politician has contributed as he has to making what was a provincial town administered by the British into a flourishing metropolis. There are no plaques to Teddy Kollek but almost everything modern that has been created in Jerusalem, and everything old that has been made worth seeing again, can be attributed to him. He was also very closely involved in setting up the Israel Museum and initiated the Spring Festival (cf. Quotations). Through his unremitting efforts Kollek, who is reckoned to be one of the most popular and progressive of Jewish politicians, has succeeded in creating a habitable and attractive city.

It is understandable that Teddy Kollek rejects fresh division of "his" city: "Sadat's idea of two sovereign powers in one city must lead to the Berlin situation. The end result of his idea would be a customs line, a police line, two legal systems. Then you get the barbed wire along the top, and then the minefields as well. That is clearly the outcome."

The son of King David (see above) and Bath-sheba, Solomon was appointed successor to the throne by his father on his deathbed. Under Solomon's rule the United Kingdom of the Israelites saw its greatest expansion and, apart from Philistäas, it stretched from the Mediterranean to the Euphrates and, in the S, to the borders of Egypt.

Solomon
(reign: 965–926 B.C.)

Although Solomon took defensive measures by re-organising the kingdom into 12 administrative divisions, served by different rotas of army officers and court officials, equipping his fighting forces with chariots and building a great many garrisons, he was also able to increase his territory by diplomatic means, particularly through his marriages: Solomon "had seven hundred wives, princesses, and three hundred concubines" (1 Kings 11:3). The increase in territory brought with it control of almost all of Arabia's trade.

The resulting riches and the yields from copper and iron extraction on the Red Sea went predominantly towards building up the capital city of Jerusalem. Here the most important building work for which Solomon was responsible was that of the Palace/Temple complex. His father, King David, had already made a start on assembling the building materials but it was Solomon who gave King Hiram of Tyre "twenty cities in the land of Galilee" for the materials he had furnished, some small indication of the immense cost of the new palace and temple, the sight of which astonished even the Queen of Sheba, herself famed for her riches (1 Kings 10; for description see A–Z, Haram esh-Sharif).

Besides his building of the Temple and all his successes in domestic and foreign policy, it is chiefly for his wisdom that Solomon has been remembered over the ages. In the Old Testament he was already known as "wiser than all men" (1 Kings 4:31) and "there came of all people to hear the wisdom of Solomon" (4:34). The authorship has been attributed to him of the Books of Proverbs and Ecclesiastes ("the words of the Preacher, the son of David") because of his unrivalled, for his time, realism in judging human issues, and, exceptional for its natural eroticism, the Song of Solomon.

Like his father David, Solomon seems to have been torn between obedience to God and sinfulness. Although David sought forgiveness, Yahweh's judgement of Solomon was never retracted because Solomon had turned to other gods.

Under the influence of his foreign wives Solomon gave himself over to the worship of Astherot, the Phoenician goddess of fertility and love, of Moloch, the Ammonite god that demanded child sacrifices (see A–Z, Valley of Kidron: Valley of Hinnom) and other foreign gods. Yahweh's punishment for this was that after Solomon the United Kingdom would be disbanded.

Solomon died after ruling for 40 years. The United Kingdom became the Northern State of Israel and the Southern State of Judah. Solomon's grave is assumed to be in the Valley of Kidron.

History of Jerusalem

Since the history of Jerusalem and Israel is dominated by the history of the Jewish people in the centuries before the birth of Christ, accounts are also given of events that are recounted in the Bible, that may be mythical or not historical, if they are of crucial importance.

c. 3000 B.C.

The Deluge, the biblical "Flood", inundates Mesopotamia, Egypt and the rest of the Middle East. This catastrophic flooding leads to extensive building of dams and canals (Nile, Euphrates, Tigris).

The change in climate that took place at the end of the Middle Stone Age had resulted in the creation of a belt of desert, so that early settlements are concentrated around rivers and oases.

1991 B.C.

Together with the Nile area, Egypt rules Nubia and Sinai peninsula and makes conquests in S Palestine, the land of Canaan (W of the River Jordan).

c. 1800 B.C.

Abraham:
Nomadic tribes led by Abram of Ur (Mesopotamia) move into the S part of Canaan. Famine forces the tribes into fertile Lower Egypt. Abram returns to Canaan a rich man and settles near Hebron. At this time he meets with Melchizedek, king of Salem (=Jerusalem according to Jewish tradition and in the view of Christian church fathers) who is "the priest of the most high God" (Genesis 14:18).

The Covenant:
Yahweh (Jehovah) makes a covenant with Abram, renaming him Abraham "for a father of many nations have I made thee. And I will make thee exceeding fruitful . . . giving thee and thy seed after thee all the land of Canaan for an everlasting possession . . . Every man child shall be circumcised at eight days old as a token of the covenant" (Genesis 17).

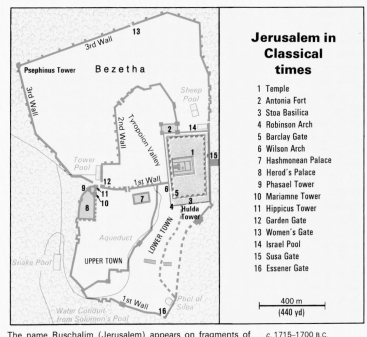

Jerusalem in Classical times

1 Temple
2 Antonia Fort
3 Stoa Basilica
4 Robinson Arch
5 Barclay Gate
6 Wilson Arch
7 Hashmonean Palace
8 Herod's Palace
9 Phasael Tower
10 Mariamne Tower
11 Hippicus Tower
12 Garden Gate
13 Women's Gate
14 Israel Pool
15 Susa Gate
16 Essener Gate

400 m
(440 yd)

The name Ruschalim (Jerusalem) appears on fragments of 14th Dynasty Egyptian tablets of curses – curses were written on tablets that were then shattered to make the curse come true.

c. 1715–1700 B.C.

"Israel":
Jacob, the son of Abraham, wrestles with a man "until the breaking of the day". The man identifies himself as God and gives Jacob the name "Israel" – he who has prevailed with God. The 12 tribes that proceed from the 12 sons of Jacob are correspondingly known as the children of Israel (Genesis 32:25 et seq.).
The concept of "Israelites" firstly applies to all 12 tribes but later also comes to distinguish between the tribe of Judah and the other tribes. After the return from Babylonian captivity the Israelites are collectively termed Jews (i.e. of Judah).

c. 1700 B.C.

Joseph:
Joseph, son of Jacob, is sold by his brothers to a caravan of Egyptian traders but rises to an influential position at the court of Lower Egypt. When Jacob's sons come to buy corn in Egypt Joseph invites them and their father to stay in Egypt. They settle in the E Nile delta.
About the same time the Hyksos, semitic Asiatic tribes, attack and conquer Egypt, thanks to their superior fighting techniques (horsedrawn chariots etc.).
The Jewish tradition allies the children of Israel with the Hyksos.

c. 1650 B.C.

21

c. 1550 B.C.	Pharaoh Ahmose drives out some of the Hyksos into Palestine. Jacob's descendants left behind in Egypt are viewed as a constant threat by the Pharaohs and are finally set to work as slaves.
from 1500 B.C.	Increased penetration by the Israelites into Palestine.
c. 1400–1300 B.C.	Abd Hiba, king of Urusalim (Jerusalem) writes to Egypt for help against attacks by a Hebrew desert tribe on the S border.
c. 1250 B.C.	Exodus from Egypt: Even after nine plagues (turning the Nile red, locusts, floods, etc.) Moses fails to persuade Pharaoh to release the Israelites from their bondage. Moses announces a tenth plague: on a certain night all the firstborn shall die. On this night in each Israelite house a whole lamb shall be roasted, its blood will be smeared on the doorposts and lintels of the houses. Shortly before midnight the God Yahweh passes through the land and "smites all the firstborn in the land of Egypt, both man and beast". The Israelite houses in which, instead of the firstborn, a lamb has been sacrificed, are passed over (origin of the feast of the Passover). In the same night the Israelites depart and Pharaoh's pursuing host is drowned in the Red Sea. The Exodus from Egypt becomes a trek over approximately 40 years through the desert of "about six hundred thousand on foot that were men, beside children" (Exodus 12:37). In the desert on Mount Sinai the Covenant with Yahweh is renewed, i.e. the laws governing social and religious life come into being: the Ten Commandments, the Ark of the Covenant (two stone tablets with the Ten Commandments), the Book of the Covenant, etc.
c. 1200 B.C.	After Moses conquers the land E of Jordan and Joshua the land W of Jordan the area is divided up among the 12 tribes. Jebus (Jerusalem), the fortified city of the Jebusites, which lies between the territories of the tribes of Judah and Benjamin cannot be taken. After the death of Moses and his successor Joshua the period of the Judges begins. The 12 tribes form a loose federation: local judges, elders and chiefs assume the functions of leaders.
after 1200 B.C.	The Philistines – seafarers who have formed the city federation of Philistäa on the coast of Palestine – and the Ammonites, who live E of the Jordan, exert considerable pressure on the 12 tribes. This leads to the tribes uniting and gradually forming one central kingdom.
c. 1050–1004 B.C.	Reign of King Saul.
1004–965 B.C.	The Prophet and Judge Samuel anoints David king of Judah. David lives first in Hebron, is later recognised by the 12 tribes as king of the United Kingdom, defeats the Philistines and storms Jebus, the hitherto impregnable fortified city of the Jebusites. The Jebusite acropolis Zion is renamed the City of David and Jerusalem is developed as the capital of the kingdom. The choice falls on this city because of its central location between Israel and Judah and its neutral status – Jebus was not allotted to any of the 12 tribes. David's city has about 2000 inhabitants in an area of about

19 sq. miles/50 sq. km. By having the Ark of the Covenant lodged there David's city also becomes the religious centre of the state.

Under Solomon, "king of peace", the United Kingdom first achieves its greatest extent. Apart from Philistäas it extended from the coast to the Euphrates and in the S to the borders of Egypt. The territorial growth brings with it control of almost all of Arabia's trade. The wealth goes predominantly into developing the capital.   964–926 B.C.

Death of Solomon and dissolution of the United Kingdom into Israel in the N and Judah in the S (capital Jerusalem).   926 B.C.

King Hezekiah's reign in the S kingdom of Judah. The springs of water (Gihon) outside the city are covered over and channelled into the city through a tunnel. Hezekiah undertakes religious reforms (destruction of the brazen serpent; possibly removal of the Ark of the Covenant).   725–697 B.C.

Destruction of Israel, the N kingdom, by Sargon II of Assyria. Most of the population are carried off to captivity in Assyria and Assyrians are settled in their place. The Samaritans result from the intermarriage of the new settlers with the remaining Israelites (Samaria is the country around the former capital of the same name of the N kingdom).
The State of Israel vanishes from the history books for more than 2500 years.   722 B.C.

The S kingdom of Judah is overthrown by Sennacherib of Assyria and Jerusalem is besieged. "Miraculous" raising of the siege (plague) and withdrawal of Sennacherib.   701 B.C.

Under King Menasseh Judah becomes a vassal state of the Assyrians.   696–642 B.C.

King Josiah purifies the land of idolatry and of the "high shrines" of the Canaanites and re-introduces the Feast of the Passover.
The Prophet Jeremiah preaches of the ruin that will inevitably befall the people unless they mend their ways.   639–609 B.C.

Nebuchadnezzar II (New Babylonian Kingdom) occupies Jerusalem, plunders the Temple and makes Judah a vassal state. After a few years, however, under King Joachim Judah again declines.   597 B.C.

Nebuchadnezzar retakes Jerusalem: destruction of Jerusalem and deportation of the Jews into Babylonian captivity.   587 B.C.

Conquest of the New Babylonian Kingdom by Cyrus the Great of Persia. The Temple vessels stolen by Nebuchadnezzar are returned to the Jews. Some of the deported Jews return from exile. They are permitted to erect a house of God in Jerusalem. Through this policy Cyrus seeks to make the Jews his allies. Jehud (Judah) becomes a Persian Province within the fifth satrapy.
Beginning of the building of the "Second Temple" under Zerubbavel, the governor appointed by the Persian king.   539 B.C.

Completion of the Second Temple.   515 B.C.

History of Jerusalem

458 B.C.

Artaxerxes I of Persia sends the Jewish priest and scribe Ezra with seven counsellors "to inquire concerning Judah and Jerusalem" (Ezra 7:14) in order to bring the Jews – who may obey the law of their God – into the Persian Empire. Ezra takes with him (newly written) parts of Moses' books of laws.

445–c. 423 B.C.

Artaxerxes sends his cupbearer Nehemiah to be governor of Jerusalem. The walls of the city are rebuilt in "52 days" (Nehemiah 2 et seq.).
After Ezra has read the book of the law of Moses the Covenant is sealed again, enjoining the observance of the laws of Moses in every detail (e.g. Sabbath), etc.

332 B.C.

Jerusalem surrenders without a fight to Alexander the Great and is granted privileges.

323 B.C.

Death of Alexander the Great and beginning of the Diadochi conflicts. After Alexander's territory has been divided up, Ptolemy becomes governor of Egypt.

305 B.C.

Ptolemy I assumes the title of (Greek) king of Egypt.

by 301 B.C.

Ptolemy I has conquered Palestine. Judah, with Jerusalem as its centre, receives a certain amount of autonomy. Friendly relations with Egypt bring prosperity to the country.
The internal administration is in the hands of the High Priest who is supported by the Council of Elders (Sanhedrin).

282 B.C.

Death of Ptolemy I. Under his successors fighting breaks out with the Seleucids over Palestine.

c. 198/195 B.C.

Palestine finally falls to the Seleucids. Antiochos III presses on with the Hellenisation of Palestine. The population is forced to worship Zeus. Tyranny results, with great bloodshed.

175 B.C.

Antiochos IV, Epiphanes "the Crazy", comes to the throne. His reign of terror is aimed at complete Hellenisation (ban on circumcision, Sabbath observance, etc.); Jerusalem is renamed Antiochia.

c. 169 B.C.

Antiochos IV is responsible for the plundering of the Temple and destruction of the holy books.

168 B.C.

The Jews are utterly deprived of all religious rights. The Priest Mattathias and his five sons organise the revolt against the Seleucid reign of terror. Mattathias' eldest son, Judas Maccabeus, assumes command of the resistance fighters.

165 B.C.

The Maccabeans seize the Temple Mount and restore the deconsecrated Temple to its former role (origin of the Feast of the Dedication of the Temple).
Mutual hostility towards the Seleucids brings about a reconciliation between Rome and Jerusalem.

152 B.C.

Jonathan Maccabeus becomes governor of Jerusalem. Discord among the Syrian Seleucids leads to successes for Jonathan.

142 B.C.

After Jonathan is murdered by the Syrian general Antiochos Theos, Simon, the last of the five Maccabean brothers, takes over the office of governor. Simon officially recognises the supreme rule of the Seleucids but at the same time effects freedom from tribute and hence independence.

Simon is installed as hereditary High Priest and Prince. The dynasty is named the Hashmoneans. 140 B.C.

Simon and two of his sons are murdered in Dok Fortress near Jericho. John Hyrcanus, the third son, escapes and follows his father in office. 134 B.C.

Conflicts between various religious groups – Sadducees, Pharisees, Essene – overshadow the otherwise largely peaceful reign of John Hyrcanus. 134–104 B.C.

John Hyrcanus designates his wife Princess and his son Aristobulus High Priest. Aristobulus, however, siezes the throne from his mother and makes himself king. He is succeeded by his brother Alexander Jannaeus. 104–103 B.C.

Alexander Jannaeus expands the kingdom but still has internal conflicts with the Pharisees, thus "diminishing the nation by 56,000 fallen, 8000 banished and 800 crucified". He ranks as the inventor of death by crucifixion. 103–76 B.C.

Alexander Jannaeus' wife Salome succeeds him on the throne. After her death her son, Hyrcanus, until then the High Priest, assumes power. His brother Aristobulus also lays claim to the throne and both turn to Rome for assistance. 76–63 B.C.

After a three-month siege (massacre, fresh damage to the Temple) the Roman general Pompey captures Jerusalem and installs Hyrcanus as High Priest. Hyrcanus becomes ethnarch (governor) but not king. This signals the end of the independent kingdom which becomes a vassal state of Rome. The ethnarchy is divided into five administrative districts, each headed by a Sanhedrin (Jewish Council of Elders). Antipatros, father of Herod the Great, becomes Hyrcanus' adviser but in fact is the power behind the throne. 63 B.C.

Antipatros becomes Procurator of Judea. His sons Herod and Phasael share in the rule. 47 B.C.

Murder of Antipatros. In the ensuing conflicts with the Hashmoneans Herod flees to Rome, Phasael commits suicide, Hyrcanus has his ears cut off and is deported (a deaf man may not be High Priest or king), the Hasmonean Antigonus makes himself king with the aid of the Parthians. 43 B.C.

The Roman Senate names Herod King of the Jews and sends him to Judea. The Jewish Sanhedrins are largely deprived of power. 40 B.C.

Herod captures Jerusalem, has Antigonus executed and begins his reign. 37 B.C.

Herod has the Temple refurbished and rebuilt. c. 20 B.C.

Death of Herod the Great. His son, Archelaus, takes the largest share of the kingdom with Jerusalem, Samaria, Judea and Idumea. 4 B.C.

Birth of Christ. c. 4 B.C.

History of Jerusalem

A.D. 6	Jews and Samaritans in Rome manage to get Herod's son Archelaus deposed. Judea is placed directly under Roman administration. A Procurator is put in charge of the province.
A.D. 26	Pontius Pilate becomes Procurator. According to non-Biblical evidence his period of office is marked by extremely harsh treatment of the Jewish population.
c. A.D. 27	Beginning of Christ's public acts.
c. A.D. 30–32	Christ is condemned to death and crucified.
A.D. 37–44	Herod Aggrippa I.
from A.D. 44	The Roman administration's emperor-worship and extremely high taxes meet with increasingly fierce resistance on the part of the Jews.
A.D. 66–70	First Jewish uprising against foreign rule by the Romans.
A.D. 70	Capture and destruction of Jerusalem by Titus, son of Emperor Vespasian.
A.D. 73	Fall of the Jewish fortress of Massada on the Dead Sea.
129	Emperor Hadrian visits the captured territory around Jerusalem and decides that the city shall be rebuilt on the Roman pattern. Hadrian's full name is Publius Aelius Hadrianus and the new city of Jerusalem is named Aelia Capitolina (Capitol=symbol of the Roman state religion). The Roman custom of ploughing a furrow around the city site before reconstruction sparks off a fresh Jewish uprising against the Romans.
132	Led by Simon bar Kokhba the insurgents capture Jerusalem and erect a temple.
135	The insurrection is suppressed. Hadrian decrees that it is death for any Jew to enter the city.
136	Flattening of the ruins of the former Jerusalem and building of the Roman city Aelia Capitolina. Buildings include two public baths, theatres, a temple of Venus, on the Temple Mount a temple to Jupiter, triumphal arches in the N and W of the inner city and an equestrian statue of Hadrian E of the temple of Jupiter. The city is laid out as a Roman colonial city, square in shape with two main streets at right-angles to one another. The cardo maximus (N–S axis) leaves the city by what is today the Damascus Gate, the decumanus (E–W axis) by the Jaffa Gate. This layout is still the same today.
138	Death of Emperor Hadrian and return of many Jews.
138–161	Under the rule of Emperor Antoninus Pius most of the anti-Jewish laws are repealed.
313	Emperor Constantine the Great's edicts of Milan (the "tolerance" edict) bring full religious freedom and identification with Christianity. This elevates the standing of Jerusalem's holy places.

Constantine becomes sole ruler of the entire Roman Empire. 324
Makarios, bishop of Jerusalem, asks him to make the city one
of the holy sites of Christendom.

The emperor's mother Helena visits Jerusalem and finds "the   *c.* 326–330
True Cross". The temple of Jupiter is demolished and a start is
made on building the Church of the Holy Sepulchre on what is
assumed to be the site of Christ's tomb.

Consecration of Church of the Holy Sepulchre.   335

Building of Eleona Church on the Mount of Olives and other   336
church-building. Jerusalem becomes a Christian city that Jews
may only enter on the anniversary of the destruction of the
Temple.

Julian Apostata becomes emperor and gives permission for the   361
Temple to be rebuilt.

Death of Emperor Julian Apostata and suspension of work on   363
the Temple.

With the division of the Roman Empire the Byzantine era begins   395
for Jerusalem.

Eudocia, wife of Emperor Theodosius II, settles in Jerusalem.   *c.* 443
She arranges for the city's fortifications to be rebuilt and
advocates that the Jews receive permission to live in
Jerusalem.
Jerusalem becomes the destination of Christian pilgrims.

Justinian I ascends the throne and church-building is resumed,   527
accompanied by persecution of the Jews.

Persian invasion: Chosroes II hands the rule of Jerusalem over   614
to the Jews since they have helped with the recapture of the
city. Many churches are destroyed.

After his victory over the Persians Emperor Herakleios I visits   629
Jerusalem. He has recovered the "True Cross", stolen by the
Persians, and enters the city with it through the Golden Gate.
Byzantine rule is re-established after the Persian interlude. The
Jews are driven out of the city.

Caliph Omar, the "Commander of the Faithful" and his desert   638
horsemen seize Jerusalem without bloodshed. The Temple
precinct, which has in the interim deteriorated into being the
town rubbish dump, is cleaned up and declared the holy
precinct of Islam. Foundation stone is laid of the El Aqsa
Mosque. 70 Jewish families are allowed to return to Jerusalem.

Muawiya is proclaimed Caliph in Jerusalem, the first of the   661
Omayyad Caliphs who rule from 661 to 750. Some of them
consider Jerusalem holier than Mecca and Medina.

Caliphate of the Abbasides who rule from Baghdad. From the   750–969
mid-9th c. the Caliphs' interest in Palestine wanes. Jerusalem
declines, the lives of its inhabitants are disrupted by feuding
between Jews, Christians and Moslems.

Foundation of opposing Fatimad Caliphate, sited in Cairo, and   969
their capture of Palestine.

971	The Turkish Seljuks take Persia and the Near East. The fighting between Fatimids and Seljuks continues until the Crusaders enter Jerusalem.
1009	The Fatimid Caliph al-Hakim has all Christian buildings, apart from the Church of the Nativity in Bethlehem, destroyed.
1095	At the urging of the Byzantine emperor, Pope Urban II calls on Christendom to wage Holy War against the infidel. This first Crusade is launched in response to acts of brutality by the Seljuks in Jerusalem.
1099	The Crusaders take Jerusalem after a one-month siege. The Jewish and Moslem inhabitants are brutally slaughtered. Jerusalem becomes the capital of a Christian kingdom under Baldwin of Bouillon. Start of intense building activity.
1187	Sultan Saladin defeats the Crusader army at Hittim and captures Jerusalem. The subsequent Crusades fail.
1228–9	Although excommunicated by the Pope, Frederick II journeys to the Holy Land. This Crusade is also a failure but by diplomatic means Frederick succeeds in obtaining withdrawal from Jerusalem, Bethlehem and other Christian sites. Temple Mount, however, remains in Moslem hands.
1244	The Khwarismic Turks (Tartars) attack Jerusalem, plunder the city, destroy the Church of the Holy Sepulchre and a bloodbath results. All attempts by the Christians to recapture Jerusalem fail; this year thus signifies the ending of the Christian Kingdom of Jerusalem.
1260	Babybars, a Mameluk, becomes Sultan. Start of extensive building work in Jerusalem (mosques, schools, administrative and residential buildings, streets, etc.).
1291	The last places held by the Crusaders are captured by the Mamelukes.
1512–20	Sultan Selim I captures Syria, Arabia and Egypt. Jerusalem is now in the hands of the Ottomans.
1520–66	Under the rule of Sultan Suleiman the Magnificent Jerusalem's water supply is improved and the walls that still stand today are erected to protect the holy places; support is given to religious and instructional establishments.
1535	Suleiman concludes the Capitulation Treaty wth François I of France – and subsequently also with other European states. Their agreement allows the European signatories protection for their citizens in Jerusalem as well as fiscal and other privileges (own jurisdiction, permission to acquire land, etc.).
1566	Death of Suleiman. Development of the city halts, the economic boom is at an end. The rule begins of the Pashas who quarrel among themselves.
1840	Beginning of Turkish rule. Jerusalem rots away and becomes a subject of dispute between the European Great Powers.

Founding, with the support of the king of Prussia, of an anglican bishopric answerable to the Archbishop of Canterbury.   1841

Pope Pius IX renews the Latin Patriarchate.   1847

Opening of the first bank.   1848

The Latin and Greek churches, and the Great Powers protecting them, squabble over the right to be custodian of the Holy Places.   1850

The Turkish Government confirms the rights of the Latin Church and guarantees the Greek Church privileges.
Emperor Napoleon III unsuccessfully lays claim to the Church of the Holy Sepulchre for France.   1852

Settlers from Württemberg found the German colony with the aim of forming an ideal Christian community in the Holy Land.   1868

German influence increases with the accession of Kaiser Wilhelm II. Growing numbers of German colonists settle in Jerusalem. Trade relations with Germany are stepped up.   1888

Opening of the railway line from Jerusalem to Jaffa.   1892

The Zionist Congress in Basle summoned by Theodor Herzl signals the start of Zionism as a political movement. Its platform is to set up a national homeland for the Jewish people in the lands of the Bible.   1897

Kaiser Wilhelm II comes to Jerusalem for the opening of the Church of the Redeemer.   1898

During the First World War Jerusalem serves as a camp for the Turkish and German armies.   from 1914

The Turks surrender to the British. General Allenby enters the Old Town on foot through the Jaffa Gate. Jerusalem becomes a military occupied city under martial law.
Balfour Declaration:
Lord Balfour, the British Foreign Secretary, in writing to Baron Rothschild, declares himself in favour of establishing a national home for the Jewish people in Palestine:
"His Majesty's Government view with favour the establishment in Palestine of a national home for the Jewish people, and will use their best endeavours to facilitate the achievement of this object, it being clearly understood that nothing shall be done which may prejudice the civil and religious rights of existing non-Jewish communities in Palestine or the rights and political status enjoyed by Jews in any other country."   1917

First anti-Jewish rioting in Palestine. Foundation of the Histadruth, the Zionist Trade Union Federation.   1920

Opening of Jerusalem's Hebrew University.   1925

A severe earthquake damages many of Jerusalem's buildings (including Church of the Holy Sepulchre, El Aqsa Mosque).   1927

Further outbreaks of anti-Jewish rioting in Palestine.   1929

McDonald White Paper: London promises Palestine's Arabs   1939 independence within ten years. Jewish immigration for the next five years is to be restricted to 75,000.

1942	Biltmore Conference in New York: the Zionists reject the McDonald White Paper and call for a Jewish army.
1946	Irgun Zwai Leumi, the terrorist organisation led by Menachem Begin, blows up the East Wing of the King David Hotel in Jerusalem (headquarters of the British administration).
1947	The General Assembly of the United Nations resolves that the country should be partitioned into a Jewish and an Arab state. Jerusalem is to have international status. The Arabs reject the resolution.
1948	General Sir Alan Cunningham is the last British soldier to leave the country. On 14 May David Ben Gurion proclaims the State of Israel (without defining the borders). Only a few days later Transjordanian units capture parts of Jerusalem's Old Town. Ceasefire agreements follow but are not observed. Both sides continue to engage in very bitter fighting.
1949	After the first elections to the Israeli Knesset David Ben Gurion becomes Prime Minister and Chaim Weizman is made President. Israel becomes a member of the United Nations. Jerusalem is declared the capital of Israel.
1953	The Knesset declares that Jerusalem "was, is and shall remain" the capital of Israel. King Hussein of Jordan lets it be known that he regards Jerusalem as the second capital of the Hashemite Kingdom and an integral part of his kingdom.
1956/1957	Israel's Sinai campaign against Egypt.
1964	The PLO, Palestine Liberation Organisation, is founded in Jerusalem headed by Dr Ahmed Shukeiry.
1965	Teddy Kollek becomes Mayor of Jerusalem. Opening of the Israel Museum.
1967	Israel begins the Six Day War and defeats Egypt. The Israeli troops occupy Sinai, the Golan Heights and the West Bank of the Jordan and annex East Jerusalem. This annexation is condemned by a special session of the United Nations.
1973	Yom Kippur War: Egypt and Syria attack Israel; the Israelis sustain considerable losses. There is an international reassessment of the Palestinian problem; the EEC Foreign Ministers call for Israeli withdrawal from the territories occupied since 1967.
1975	American mediation secures military withdrawal agreements between Israel and Egypt and Israel and Syria.
1976	Jews seek to pray on Moslem Haram esh-Sharif, the former Temple Mount. Israeli soldiers break up a Moslem counter-demonstration. A lower court gives the Jews the right to pray on Haram esh-Sharif (this is forbidden for Orthodox Jews since it is not clear where the Holy of Holies of the former temple was sited). The Supreme Court of Justice reverses this judgement: Jews are not entitled to pray on Haram esh-Sharif.

After the success at the polls of his right-wing Likud block,   1977
Menachem Begin forms a coalition with Israel's religious
parties and becomes the new Prime Minister.
President Sadat of Egypt addresses the Knesset.

Signing of the Camp David Agreement between Israel, Egypt   1978
and the USA.
In Oslo Menachem Begin, the Israeli Prime Minister, receives
the Nobel Peace Prize. Sadat, with whom he shares the Prize,
sends a representative.

Signing of a Peace Treaty between Israel and Egypt.   1979

Opening of the borders between Israel and Egypt and   1980
resumption of diplomatic relations. On 29 July the UN General
Assembly demands that Israel finally withdraws from the
occupied territories, including East Jerusalem. The next day the
Knesset declares Jerusalem in its entirety the capital of Israel.

About 5000 survivors of the Nazi Holocaust meet in Jerusalem.   1981
Menachem Begin sees his position as Prime Minister
reaffirmed following fresh elections.

Israel hands back to Egypt the parts of Sinai which have been   1982
occupied since 1967.
Israeli troops invade the Lebanon with the aim of annihilating
the PLO. Entry into West Beirut which is evacuated by the
PLO.
Zionist World Congress in Jerusalem.

Chaim Herzog becomes the new President. Israel and the   1983
Lebanon sign a treaty to end the state of war.
Menachem Begin resigns as Prime Minister to be succeeded by
Yitzhak Shamir.

A large demonstration in Jerusalem demands the withdrawal of   1984
Israel from the Lebanon and the adoption of a settlement policy
in the occupied territories.
Lebanon confirms the agreement of May 1983 with Israel for
the withdrawal of troops.
In July new elections to the Knesset result in no absolute
majority. Formation of a coalition between the Likut block
(Shamir) and the Labour Party (Peres), with alternating prime
ministers.

Quotations

From a 19th c. travel journal: Arnold C. Brackman
"Jerusalem itself was full of religious fanatics and charlatans. "The Dream of Nineveh"
The constant quarrelling and rivalries between the various   (1978)
religious communities over the control of the Holy Places
offended Laylard's Christian sentiments. Shortly before Easter,

he was dismayed to learn, the Egyptian troops had to be summoned to the Church of the Holy Sepulchre to keep the peace between the warring groups. Most at odds were the Roman Catholic and the Orthodox churches, manipulated by France and Russia, thus ushering in those disputes which led to the Crimean War.

"Mitford was shocked by the carnival atmosphere in this place. 'On the Via Dolorosa', he wrote to his mother, '. . . they show you a mark in the wall where Christ is supposed to have leant his cross!' But he remarked that the wall was only 600 years old, and had therefore been built 1200 years after the event . . ."

D. Bednarz/M. Lüders
"Palestine Protocol" (1981)

From an interview with A. A. Diab, leader until 31.12.1980 of the white-collar workers at East Jerusalem's Electricity Company, which was nationalised on 1.1.1981:

"When my wife and I go shopping in the modern part of Jerusalem and then somewhere there is an outbreak of violence, fighting or a bomb goes off, we are immediately arrested by the police although we have nothing to do with it. But even before the police arrest us, we are harassed by passers-by. Why? Because we are Palestinians. That doesn't only happen to me and my family. If there is any suspicion of a bomb somewhere the police arrest Arabs because they are Arabs. Israel is mistaken if it thinks that by doing this it can stifle or change the Palestinians' attitude. Every day more and more Palestinians believe that there will be a Palestinian State. Since 1967 my brother has been in prison because he is actively campaigning for an Arab Jerusalem. But if Rabbi Kahane wants to make the Arab Ramallah Jewish that only upsets a few Israelis. The Israelis may have destroyed my house but I have rebuilt it. Now I should like a life free of restraint for my brother, my wife, my children and myself."

Theodor Herzl
(2.5.1860–3.7.1904)
"Diaries"

"When I remember thee in days to come, O Jerusalem, it will not be with delight. The musty deposits of two thousand years of inhumanity, intolerance, and foulness lie in your reeking alleys. If Jerusalem is ever ours, and if I were still able to do anything about it, I would begin by cleaning it up. I would clear out everything that is not sacred, set up workers' houses beyond the city, empty and tear down the filthy rat-holes, burn all the non-sacred ruins, and put the bazaars elsewhere. Then, retaining as much of the old architectural style as possible, I would build an airy, comfortable, properly sewered, brand new city around the Holy Places."

St Jerome, father of the
Latin Church (c. 347–420)

"Until this very day . . . it is forbidden to citizens not of the faith to come to Jerusalem . . . they may only come there to lament, and for the right to weep over the ruins of their house they must pay. At no time whatsoever may they weep gratis."

Martin Kabatnik
Bohemian monk
(1491–2 in Israel)

"The Christians and the Jews are lacking in everything and are in a pitiful situation. There are only few Christians but many Jews. A Jew whose house collapses may not build a new one in its place but must buy the land again from the previous owners and at a high price. Christians and Jews go around in Jerusalem as do beggars in our own country. They may not wear any good clothing. Despite all the affliction and oppression inflicted upon them by the non-Jews the Jews refuse to leave the place."

Theodor Herzl

Selma Lagerlöf

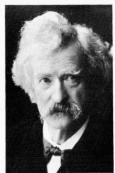

Mark Twain

"Frank Sinatra is only one of the many gifted entertainers who have been to Jerusalem since I became Mayor. I am always trying to attract people here who are known not only for their talent but who also have the corresponding charisma. These visits are important to counteract the widespread publicity the current terrorist attacks in Jerusalem are receiving. Since a visit by Frank Sinatra or Elizabeth Taylor attracts almost as much attention from the media as a bombing, their presence in Jerusalem demonstrates to the people abroad that they too can come here free of care and that life in Jerusalem is not dominated by outbreaks of terrorism or tension between Arabs and Jews. Cultivating Jerusalem's image abroad and the psychological atmosphere in the city is as much a part, to my mind, of the general plan for Jerusalem as building plans and development of projects. Although it also has its roots in the past, Jerusalem is no museum and we shall strain every nerve to ensure that for the citizen as for the visitor it remains equally open and full of life."

Teddy Kollek
"A Life for Jerusalem"
(1980)

"There was truly still a mass of people who maintained that they could best stand the summer in Jerusalem itself. Although they admitted that the city was crowded and contained far too many people, they still thought that since it was perched on the crest of the long mountainous ridge that stretched the length of Palestine not even the slightest breeze, from whichever quarter, could pass through the country without its refreshing airs wafting as far as the Holy City.
"But whatever may have been Jerusalem's relation to the much vaunted winds and the gentle mountain airs, it still also managed to heat up quite enough. People slept on the roofs at night and shut themselves indoors during the day; they had to content themselves with the foul-smelling drinking water that was collected during the winter rains in underground cisterns and that one was always afeared would run dry. The slightest wind filled the air with thick clouds of chalk dust and if anyone went walking on the white roads outside the city their feet sank right down into the thick white dust."

Selma Lagerlöf
(20.11.1858–16.3.1940)
"Jerusalem"

Quotations

Mark Twain (Samuel
Langhorne Clemens)
(30.11.1835–21.4.1901)
"Innocents Abroad"

"At last, away in the middle of the day, ancient bits of walls and crumbling arches began to line the way – we toiled up one more hill, and every pilgrim and every sinner swung his hat on high! Jerusalem!

"Perched on its enternal hills, white and domed and solid, massed together and hooped with high grey walls, the venerable city gleamed in the sun. So small! Why, it was no larger than an American village of four thousand inhabitants, and no larger than an ordinary Syrian city of thirty thousand. Jerusalem numbers only fourteen thousand people.

"We could recognise the Tower of Hippicus, the Mosque of Omar, the Damascus Gate, the Mount of Olives, the Valley of Jehoshaphat, the Tower of David, and the Garden of Gethsemane – and dating from these landmarks could tell very nearly the localities of many others we were not able to distinguish . . .

"Just after noon we entered these narrow, crooked streets, by the ancient and famed Damascus Gate, and now for several hours I have been trying to comprehend that I am actually in the illustrious old city where Solomon dwelt, where Abraham held converse with the Deity, and where walls still stand that witnessed the spectacle of the Crucifixion.

"The population of Jerusalem is composed of Moslems, Jews, Greeks, Latins, Armenians, Syrians, Copts, Abyssinians, Greek Catholics, and a handful of Protestants. One hundred of the latter sect are all that dwell now in this birthplace of Christianity. The nice shades of nationality comprised in the above list, and the languages spoken by them are altogether too numerous to mention. It seems to me that all the races and colours and tongues of the earth must be represented among the fourteen thousand souls that dwell in Jerusalem. Rags, wretchedness, poverty and dirt – those signs and symbols that indicate the presence of Moslem rule more surely than the crescent-flag itself – abound.

"Lepers, cripples, the blind and the idiotic assail you on every hand, and they know but one word of but one language apparently – the eternal 'baksheesh'. To see the number of maimed, malformed and diseased humanity that throng the holy places and obstruct the gates, one might suppose that the ancient days had come again, and that the angel of the Lord was expected to descend at any moment to stir the waters of Bethesda."

Marlies Menge "The Negev
Is Desert Enough" (1981)

"In 4000-year-old Jerusalem the past and present of the country had caught up with us again. Thanks to a friend . . . in the half day left to us I saw at least what was of most importance. She led me through the narrow Arab alleyways and the new Jewish quarter to the Wailing Wall (where our bags were checked) and to the Church of the Holy Sepulchre, the church of Christ the peacemaker, in which six sects wage their cold war.

"In the ghetto of the orthodox Jews I felt like an extra in a medieval film, between the black-clad men with their ringlets on their temples, the children in their old-fashioned clothing, which in this summer heat bared only their head and hands to the air. We were spat at by furious men because our arms were not covered down to the wrists. My friend, who was familiar with the locality, took me up the Mount of Olives because she wanted to show me the truly golden light of the evening over the city so that I would understand why here everyone felt nearer to their god than anywhere else."

"Always when I visited Jerusalem I went into the Al-Aqsa Mosque, on the side of which is a small prayer room which the Franks (= Crusaders) have made into a church. As soon as I set foot in the Al-Aqsa Mosque, in which the Templars were to be found, with whom I was befriended, they cleared this small prayer room for me so that I could say my prayers.

"When I entered there again one day, spake 'Allâhu akbar' and set myself down to pray, a Frank fell upon me, laid hold of me, turned my face to the East and shouted 'that is how to pray!'. A couple of Templars hurried to him, seized hold of him and removed him from me. I resumed my prayers. However, the Frank seized upon a moment when the Templars were not looking to fall upon me once more, turned my face towards the East and cried out 'that is how to pray!'. The Templars came back in again and got him outside. They begged my pardon and said 'that is a stranger who has only arrived today from the land of the Franks and has not yet seen anyone who does not face the East in prayer'. – 'I have prayed enough', responded I and went outside, amazed at how the colour had drained from the devil's face, how he had shaken and conducted himself at the sight of someone who directed his prayers towards Mecca."

Usâma ibn Munqidh (4.7.1095–16.11.1188) "A Life at War with the Crusader Armies"

"I write you this letter from the Holy City Jerusalem. Great is the suffering, and great is the devastation, and the holier the place, the greater the devastation. Jerusalem is more ravaged than the rest of the country . . .

"There are dwelling here some two thousand, three hundred of them Christians, but no Jews . . . Now there are only two Brothers there, dyers, who buy their dyes from the government . . . and we found a dilapidated house . . . and made it into a synagogue; for the city has no ruler and anyone can, if he will, take a ruin. And we were ready to repair the house . . . and they sent already to Nablus, to fetch the scrolls of the law, which were in Jerusalem but had been taken away when the Tartars came. And now they have set up a synagogue where they shall pray. For there are always people coming to Jerusalem, men and women from Damascus and Aleppo and from every part of the country, to see the Temple and to weep."

Rabbi Nachmanides (c. 1194–1270)

"Connoisseurs of Israel had already advised me in Hamburg 'don't change your money at the Airport in Lod; just change enough for a taxi to Jerusalem'; I should change money in the Old Town of Jerusalem but, whatever I did, not at a bank, but with the moneychangers. There I would get more, much more; they would have a better rate.

"It's possible that they have that for Israel connoisseurs. They didn't for me. I gave a hundred Marks, as much as I had changed at the airport. And then I waited for the notes I should get. The moneychanger started counting them out. When he got to 80% of what I had got from the bank at Lod he stopped and pushed me the notes . . . It took a long time, and a lot of trouble, to get my share up to at least 90%. Then I gave up.

"During this time I had been wondering what I could do to him. One thing was certain: I couldn't overturn his table; it was a counter. The Jerusalem moneychangers, I thought, had already tried in Jesus' time to cheat the visitors to the city. Had they also paid him a poor rate of exchange? . . . Had Jesus driven out the moneychangers for that reason and overturned their tables? No, for him it was about something different."

Gerhard Prause "The Little World of Jesus Christ" (1981)

Quotations

Zechariah
(6th c. B.C.)

Chapter 14:1–5:

"Behold, the day of the Lord cometh, and thy spoil shall be divided in the midst of thee.

"For I will gather all nations against Jerusalem to battle; and the city shall be taken, and the houses rifled, and the women ravished; and half of the city shall go forth into captivity, and the residue of the people shall not be cut off from the city.

"Then shall the Lord go forth, and fight against those nations, as when he fought in the day of battle.

"And his feet shall stand in that day upon the mount of Olives, which is before Jerusalem on the east, and the mount of Olives shall cleave in the midst thereof toward the east and toward the west, and there shall be a very great valley; and half of the mountain shall remove toward the north, and half of it toward the south.

"And ye shall flee to the valley of the mountains; for the valley of the mountains shall reach unto Azal: yea, ye shall flee, like as ye fled from before the earthquake in the days of Uzziah king of Judah: and the Lord my God shall come, and all the saints with thee."

Muriel Spark "The
Mandelbaum Gate" (1965)

"He was approaching the end of the Orthodox Jewish quarter, and had turned into a street at the end of which rattled the modern state. There, small shops burst their sides with business, large cars streaked along the highway, and everywhere the radio sets told the news in several tongues ranging from Hebrew to that of the B.B.C., or attacked the hot air with oriental jazz. Up there at the end of this orthodox street, it was said, the Orthodox Jews would gather on a Saturday morning, piously to stone the passing motor-cars, breakers of the Sabbath. And across the street, streamers stretched from building to building, bearing the injunction in Hebrew, French and English:

DAUGHTERS OF ISRAEL, OBSERVE MODESTY
IN THESE STREETS!

"This Freddy assumed to be for the benefit of any tourist-woman who might, for some mad reason, wish to walk in this Orthodox Jewish quarter wearing shorts or a low-cut sun dress."

Jerusalem from A to Z

Abu Gosh

The village of Abu Gosh is about 8 miles/13 km W of Jerusalem on the Tel Aviv road. Its most important building is a Crusader church which has survived almost intact.

Abu Gosh is said to be the Qiryat Tearim of the Old Testament, where the Ark of the Covenant rested for 20 years before being taken to Jerusalem (1 Samuel 7:1–2). Today the Church of Our Lady of the Ark of the Covenant, dominating the landscape with its statue of Mary, stands on the site of the Old Testament village.

In the 8th c. a hospice was built in the valley, near the spring which has now been made a reservoir. In 1142 Crusaders built the fortified church over the spring, identifying the site as the Emmaus of the New Testament. 300 years after the Crusaders withdrew El Qubeiba (see entry) was declared to be the true Emmaus.

Next to the Church of St Anne in Jerusalem (see entry) the church of Abu Gosh is the best-preserved example of Crusader architecture. With walls that are up to 13 ft/4 m thick, the church, which is 66 ft/20 m long and 49 ft/15 m wide and has a nave and two aisles, resembles a fortress. Its massive exterior accords with its stark but impressive interior, decorated only by much-faded frescoes. At the N entrance is a Roman inscription recalling "Fratensis", the Tenth Legion.

Buses
From the main bus station in Yafo Road

Location
8 miles/13 km W

Alexandra Hospice

E8

The Alexandra Hospice contains the church of the Russian Orthodox community. During the building of the church (19th c.) sections were uncovered of the Second Wall which protected the N side of the city in the time of Herod I. This seemed to indicate that the Holy Tomb in the Church of the Holy Sepulchre (see entry) was outside the city walls of the time, grounds for considering it to be where Christ was buried. Also visible are the much-modified and restored remains of a triumphal arch from the time of Hadrian. This may at one time have stood in front of the entrance to the forum of Aelia Capitolina during the Roman period.

Location
Old Town, opposite the Church of the Redeemer

Buses
1, 12, 27

Opening times
Mon.–Thurs. 9 a.m.–3 p.m.

Antonia Fort

See Via Dolorosa.

Armenian Quarter

E7/8

The heart of the Armenian Quarter is a walled enclave in the SW of the Old Town. As used to happen with every quarter of Jerusalem, here the main gate is still locked in the evening. The showpiece of the quarter is its Church of St James.
The Church of Armenia is one of the oldest-established

Location
Armenian Patriarchate Road (SW Old Town)

Buses
1, 13, 19, 20, 23

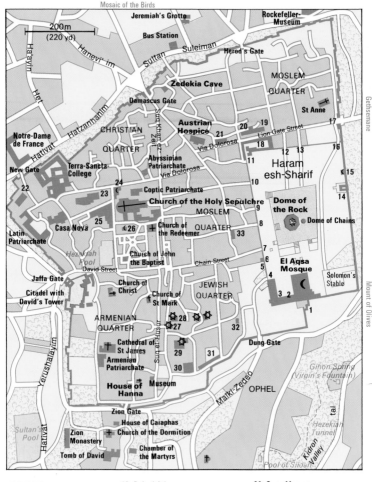

Old Town

1 Double Gate
2 White Mosque
3 Islamic Museum
4 Gate of the Moroccans
5 Wailing Wall
6 Wailing Wall – Synagogue
7 Gate of the Chain
8 Gate of the Cotton Merchants
9 Iron Gate
10 Bab en Nadhir (Nazir)
11 Bab el Ghawanima

12 Bab el Atim
13 Bab Hitta
14 Golden Gate
15 Throne of Solomon
16 Bab el Asbat
17 Lion Gate (St Stephen's Gate)
18 El Omariye School
19 Chapel of the Flagellation
20 Judgement Chapel
21 Church of the Sisters of Zion
22 Jesuit College
23 Greek Patriarch's Palace
24 El Khanqa Mosque
25 Monastery of Constantine

26 Omar Mosque
27 Ramban Synagogue
28 Hurva Synagogue
29 Synagogue Complex:
   Yohanan ben
   Zakkai Synagogue
   Eliah Hanavi Synagogue
   Emtzai Synagogue
   Istanbul Synagogue
30 Metivta Yeshiva
31 Yeshival Hakotel
32 Porat Yosef Yeshiva
33 Hammam el Ein

Christian churches. Its missionaries were supposed to be the Apostles Judas Thaddaus and Bartholomew but its true founder is thought to have been St Gregory the Enlightener (Grigor Lusavorich) who visited Armenia as early as the 3rd or 4th c. when he converted the king of Armenia to Christianity which then became the country's established religion.

Church of St James (Cathedral)

The Church of St James, with its own monastery, is in the centre of the Armenian Quarter and is the focus for almost all the buildings in the quarter.

Opening times
Mon.–Fri. 3–3.30 p.m., Sat. and Sun. 2.30–3.15 p.m.

The fountain at the entrance to the monastery commemorates the accession to the throne of Sultan Abdulhamid. The Armenian Patriarchate is on the right of the courtyard.

A notable feature at the entrance to the church is an ancient wooden board known as the "nakus" (gong), which is struck in the place of a bell. In 1823 the only bell in the whole of Jerusalem was a handbell in the Franciscan monstery. The bells now in the tower date only from 1840. As late as the end of the 19th c. the nuns of the Russian convent had to carry their bell themselves from the harbour in Jaffa to the Mount of Olives (see entry), since the Moslem workmen refused to move a bell. According to tradition the church was built on the spot where in A.D. 44 Herod Agrippa I had the Apostle James the Greater put to the sword (Acts 12:2). There was a monastery of St James here as early as the 7th c. and in the 12th c. the Crusaders joined with the Armenians in building the present church on Georgian foundations.

The Armenian Quarter: a walled enclave in the Old Town

Interior

Four square pillars, adorned with blue tiles from Spain, support the large dome of the aisled church above which rises a hexagonal star-shaped tower. In the 15th–17th c. the Armenian community prospered because of generous gifts from Spain owing to the links forged by their common veneration of St James, whose relics are kept in Santiago de Compostela.

A richly decorated chapel in the N aisle marks the spot where St James is said to have been beheaded.

Next to the Chapel of St James are the sacristy and other rooms belonging to the Armenian Patriarchate. These are the oldest parts of the church but are not open to visitors since they contain the treasury of the Patriarchate.

In the choir is the Cathedra of the Armenian Patriarchs. The ancient chair next to it is known as "St James' Chair".

As the church has no electric light and little light reaches it from outside, the atmosphere is one of solemn devotion.

Leaving the Church of St James and passing the houses of Armenian families and pilgrims' hostels one reaches the library and the Museum of Armenian Art and History.

Museum of Armenian Art and History

Opening times
Mon.–Sat. 10 a.m.–4.30 p.m.

The Museum of Armenian Art and History was founded by Helen and Edward Mardigian and is therefore also known as the Mardigian Museum. Here on two floors are displayed Armenian arts and crafts, ritual objects and historical documents.

Interior of the "House of Annas" church in the Armenian Quarter

House of Annas

The "House of Annas" church dates back to 1300 when it was
built as the "Church of the Angels".
Annas, who was the father-in-law of the High Priest Caiaphas
and was dismissed by the Roman Procurator, was the high
priest before whom Jesus was taken after his capture. Annas
had Jesus beaten and then sent him bound to Caiaphas (John
18:12 et seq.). The angels, it is said, covered their faces so they
would not have to watch.
The visitor first enters a porch in which stands a fountain. To the
right a fine doorway leads into the church. In the left aisle is a
chapel which commemorates Jesus being mocked by Annas.

Monastery of the Olive Tree

The adjacent Monastery of the Olive Tree is named after the
fenced-in tree that stands close by the house of Annas.
Tradition has it that Jesus was bound to this tree the night after
he was taken prisoner.
A few paces further on at the NE corner of the church is the
stone that would "cry out" if the Disciples held their peace. (Cf.
the "Crying Stones" near the Dominus Flevit church on the
Mount of Olives – see entry.)

Ascension Chapel

See Mount of Olives

Bethany

See Mount of Olives

Bethesda Pool

See Church of St Anne

** Bethlehem (Beit Lahm)

Bethlehem, the birthplace of Jesus, is in the Israeli-occupied
Arab part of Palestine. Parts of it still look like a true eastern
country town with Arab markets, colourful bazaars and farmers
driving their sheep out to graze.
For the Arabs the town's name means "House of Meat" (Beit
Lahm); to the Hebrews "lehm" means "bread", hence the usual
interpretation is "House of Bread". Both names, Hebrew and
Arabic, refer to the fertility of this region and to the farming and
stockbreeding which used to be the main occupation of its
people.
The slopes of the hills are planted with vines, almond, olive and
fig trees. In Genesis (35:19) Bethlehem is called Ephrat, "Land
of Fruit", a name that later came to refer to the whole of the

Bus
From the Damascus Gate

Taxis
From the Damascus and
Jaffa Gates

Location
8 miles/13 km S

Bethlehem: the traditional birthplace of Jesus

district around Bethlehem. The landscape is at its most beautiful in the spring when the almond trees are in bloom. In summer everything is parched with the heat and the countryside matches the nearby desert.

Today a large share of Bethlehem's 27,000 inhabitants make their living from tourism. The manufacture and sale of souvenirs are major sources of income. Saints' portraits, figures of all kinds made out of mother-of-pearl, wood and "Dead Sea stone" (bituminous limestone), embroidered blouses, Crusader jerkins, etc., are on offer at every turn.

For all pilgrims to Bethlehem the main attraction is the Church of the Nativity. Other sights include the Grotto of the Milk, the tomb of Rachel and Beit Sahur, the "Village of the Shepherds". Not far from Bethlehem are the Pools of Solomon (see entry), and the Elijah Monastery on the road from Jerusalem which is worth a visit.

Biblical history

Genesis mentions "the way to Ephrat, which is Bethlehem" (35:19), so a settlement must have existed here at a very early date.

Information on the period of the Judges, three generations before King David (1004–965 B.C.) is a little more precise. The Book of Ruth, which traces the line of David's ancestry, provides a good insight into the life of Bethlehem's peasants and landowners and into the marriage customs of the time. The central figure is the widow Ruth who, when gleaning corn in the field belonging to Boaz, claimed him for her husband and bore him Obed, the grandfather of David (see p. 49, Beit Sahur, Ruth's field).

Bethlehem enters the chronicles of history with David, who was born here and was originally a shepherd before being

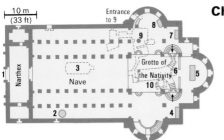

Church of the Nativity
Bethlehem

1 Entrance
2 Font
3 Mosaic Floor
4 Altar of the Circumcision
5 Main Altar
6 Iconostasis
7 Altar of the Three Kings
8 Altar of the Virgin
9 Grotto of the Innocents
10 Altar of the Manger

anointed king by Samuel (1 Samuel 16). His grandson Rehoboam (king of Judah 926–910 B.C.) turned Bethlehem into a fortified city (2 Chronicles 11:5–6). The return from the Babylonian Captivity (c. 539 B.C.) saw the resettlement of this fertile area (Ezra 2:21).

Bethlehem's main claim to fame, however, is as the place where Jesus was born (Matthew 2:1; Luke 2:4–7). Possibly this event may have been "transposed" here, for the prophet Micah had proclaimed that the Messiah, the new Prince of Israel, would be born in the princely city (i.e. the City of David) (Matthew 2:5–6; cf. John 7:40 et seq. and Nathanael's question, "Can there any good thing come out of Nazareth?", John 1:46). Otherwise Jesus is known as the Nazarene, "he who hails from Nazareth", but Matthew also managed to trace this back to a prophecy (2:23). In fact Matthew Chapter 2 is devoted to tracing back the Holy Family's places of origin to prophecies. It is only here, too, that one finds the atrocity of the Massacre of the Innocents which is also derived from a prophecy (2:16 et seq.).

In the post-Christian era the history of Bethlehem basically coincides with the history of the Church of the Nativity.

Church of the Nativity

The Church of the Nativity is one of the few buildings remaining virtually intact from the early Christian era. Despite damage, restoration and other building work it has survived the centuries in an almost unaltered state.

In 326, at the urging of his mother Helena (see Introduction, Famous People), a tireless advocate for building new churches, Emperor Constantine had a basilica built over what was assumed to be Jesus' birthplace. The people of Bethlehem knew that the Messiah had been born in a grotto among trees on the outskirts of the village (Origenes). The trees were felled, and the octagonal E apse of Constantine's building was built above the grotto.

History of the building

Grove of Adonis

After the suppression of the second Jewish uprising (A.D. 135) Emperor Hadrian erected a shrine in the grove of trees over the grotto: this shrine was dedicated to Adonis who was loved by the Greek goddess Aphrodite whom the Romans called Venus. Handsome young Adonis was killed by a boar while out hunting whereupon Persephone, goddess of the Underworld, granted Aphrodite's wish that he could spend six months of each year on earth. The annual death and rebirth of Adonis became synonymous with the natural cycle of withering and renewal that is so typical of Bethlehem's type of landscape.

Not long after Constantine built his church Jerome (*c.* 347–420) made his famous translation of the Bible in one of the grottos under the church (see p. 49, Jerome's study). He complained in a letter, "The most hallowed spot on earth was overshadowed by a grove to Adonis. And there, within the grotto, where the baby Messiah cried, they used to lament Venus' paramour."

Justinian's Church of the Nativity
Samaritans badly damaged Constantine's basilica in the course of a revolt in 529. Emperor Justinian I (527–565) ordered the building to be demolished and had the present Church of the Nativity built in its place with its central nave and double aisles on either side.

When the Persians invaded in 614 they spared the Church of the Nativity because, presumably, they believed they recognised their own forebears in the faces of the "Three Wise Men from the East" in the pediment mosaic.

In 638 Caliph Omar, on a visit to Bethlehem, ordered that the S transept be given to the Moslems as a place of worship. The peaceful coexistence of Christians and Moslems was also instrumental in saving the church from destruction when the Fatimid Caliph El Hakim ordered all the other Christian sites to be destroyed (1009).

In 1099 Count Tancred, a S Italian Norman, took Bethlehem for the Crusaders. On Christmas Day 1100 Baldwin I of Boulogne

Nave of the Church of the Nativity in Bethlehem

Birthplace of Christ, the Prince of Peace

was crowned king of Jerusalem in the Church of the Nativity. His successor, Baldwin II of Le Bourg was also crowned here (1118).

The Crusaders built a monastery on the N side of the church and surrounded the buildings with massive walls and, until the end of the Latin Kingdom (1187), there was a constant flow of pilgrims. Bethlehem became rich. The walls of the church were clad with white marble and mosaics on a gold ground were added. The floor was covered with polychrome marble and the cedarwood roof was covered with lead. Marble and mosaics also decorated the walls of the Grotto of the Nativity.

The church fell into decay after the withdrawal of the Crusaders, particularly when the country was ruled by the Turks. This was exacerbated by the conflicts between the Orthodox Greeks and the Franciscans over the ownership of the shrine (see p. 46, Grotto of the Nativity).

In 1810 the Armenians also managed to gain a foothold in the church. The status quo (see Church of the Holy Sepulchre), a settlement of proprietorial rights in 1757, failed to prevent bitter and sometimes violent confrontations.

The church was badly damaged as a result of the earthquake in 1834 and a fire in 1869. Safety checks carried out by the British Mandate Authority in 1933 revealed that all it needed was a few wooden struts to prevent its imminent collapse.

The paved rectangular square in front of the church includes part of the earlier atrium and the openings of three cisterns are visible.

Courtyard

Behind the NE wall is the Franciscan monastery. In the S the courtyard is bordered by the Armenian monastery. The Greek Orthodox monastery lies to the SE of the church.

Of the three original entrances into the narthex two have been walled up. Over the central portal one can still see the frieze dating from Justinian's time and the arch inserted by the Crusaders. In the 16th c. the headroom of the entrance was reduced to only 4 ft/1·2 m to prevent the Mamelukes from riding on horseback into the church.

Narthex

The Justinian narthex extends over the width of the church (87·2 ft/26·6 m) and is divided into three by walls dating from different eras. Here, too, as in the façade, only the centre portal is open. The carvings with inscriptions in Arabic and Armenian are the remains of a wooden door donated in 1227.

Interior

Four rows each of 11 monolithic white-veined red sandstone columns with white marble capitals divide the church into a nave and four side aisles. The columns, which are 20 ft/6 m in height, are painted with a coat-of-arms, rosettes, Greek crosses and frescoes of saints, with their names in either Latin or Greek. The bases are hidden from view because the level of the floor has been raised.

The 5th c. mosaic floor (nave, N choir) is also concealed, but the Greek monks, on request, remove the boards that cover it. The roof dates from the 14th c. and was restored in 1842. Only fragments of the many magnificent wall mosaics (8th and 12th c.) remain. The most visible ones are in the N transept (Doubting Thomas, the Ascension).

The octagonal baptismal font in the S aisle dates from the Justinian period. This is where the Three Wise Men are said to have watered their mounts.

Choir

The large choir is directly above the Grotto of the Nativity. Facing the apse of the nave is the richly decorated high altar (Greek Orthodox), with, S of it, the Altar of the Circumcision, also Greek Orthodox.

N of the high altar is the Armenian Altar of the Three Kings where, according to legend, the Three Wise Men alighted from their horses.

In the N transept, which also belongs to the Armenians, the altar in the apse is dedicated to Our Lady. The door opposite leads to the Church of St Catherine (see p. 48).

Grotto of the Nativity

Steps on each side of the inner choir lead down into the rectangular Grotto of the Nativity. The room, lit by 53 lamps, is 40 ft/12 m long and 10 ft/3 m wide, and may have been used as cattle shelter in bad weather.

The floor in front of the altar is of white marble. On the star is the inscription HIC DE VIRGINE MARIA JESUS CHRISTUS NATUS EST ("Here Jesus Christ was born of the Virgin Mary") and the date 1717.

Roman Catholics affixed a silver star on this spot in 1717 but in 1847 it was stolen by Greek Orthodox. In 1852 Napoleon III became emperor of the French, proclaimed himself the successor to the Crusader king Louis IX and protector of the Catholics in the Holy Land and declared, unsuccessfully, that

The Roman Catholic Church of St Catherine in Bethlehem ▶

the Church of the Nativity was French territory. The Greek Orthodox were under the protection of the Russian tsar and they tried to drive the Roman Catholics out of the church. In 1853, however, the Turks forced them to replace the star that they had stolen. Shortly afterwards came the outbreak of the Crimean War (1853–6).

The star of Bethlehem that guided the Three Wise Men caused Johannes Kepler, court astronomer to the esoterically minded Duke Rudolf II, to speculate on the actual year of Christ's birth. He concluded it was 7 B.C. because of the special conjunction at that time of Saturn and Jupiter.

Grotto of the Manger

From the Grotto of the Nativity steps lead into the Roman Catholic Grotto of the Manger containing the Altar of the Manger. According to Petrus Comestor's Historia Scholastica (12th c.) Mary, because of her poverty, laid the Baby on hay in a manger, and the ox and the ass refrained from eating the hay which, subsequently, the Dowager Empress Helena is supposed to have taken to Rome.

The other grottos under the choir of the Church of the Nativity are reached through the Church of St Catherine.

Church of St Catherine and cloister

A door in the apse of the N transept of the Church of the Nativity (see above, choir) leads to the Roman Catholic Church of St Catherine (19th c.). The medieval cloister is particularly worth seeing. It was restored in 1948 by A. Barluzzi but reincorporating the ancient columns and capitals. Here, too, can be seen the remains of the walls of Jerome's monastery and, to the W, masonry dating from the time of Constantine and Justinian.

Grotto of the Innocents

A medieval entrance in the N right-hand aisle of St Catherine's Church leads to a number of grottos that, although linked with the Grotto of the Nativity, are not accessible from it.

The first grotto, the Chapel of the Innocents, commemorates the supposed cruel slaughter of the children of Bethlehem by Herod the Great. The only record of this is in St Matthew's gospel but since it accords with the literary cliché of the miraculous "Rescue of the Hero as a Child" (an angel warns Mary and Joseph to flee to Egypt) it was eagerly seized upon – and accredited as historical fact. Herod the Great received the doubtful distinction of being one of the cruellest men in the history of the world. He was depicted in countless plays as this "murderous brute" and "maniacal paranoid"; the very titles speak for themselves: "Herod the Child-Murderer" (Andreas Gryphius), "The Greatest Monster the World Has Known" (Calderón de la Barca), "Herod the Bloodthirsty" (Hans Sachs), etc.

A medieval mnemonic verse attributes a particular murder to each of the Herods: ASCALONITA NECIT PUEROS/ANTIPA JOHANNEM/AGRIPPA JACOBUM CLAUDENS IN CAR-CERE PETRUM: "Ascalonita (=Herod I) murdered the boys, (Herod) Antipas murdered John, (Herod) Agrippa murdered James and incarcerated Peter". See also Introduction, Famous People: Herod I.

Chapel of St Jospeh

Next to the Chapel of the Innocents is a chapel dedicated to St Joseph, the husband of Mary.

Paula, a patrician Roman widow, with her daughter Julia, toured the Holy Land in the 4th c. Here they joined the circle of ascetics around St Jerome and Paula founded a number of hospices, etc.

One of the caves is thought to be where St Jerome, the most learned of the fathers of the Church, wrote the Vulgate, for Catholics the only authorised Latin translation of the Bible until the present century. (It is currently undergoing a revision.)

Study and Grave of St Jerome

Another of the tombs is said to be the final resting-place of St Eusebius, who headed the monastery after the death of St Jerome.

Tomb of St Eusebius

A door in the apse of the S transept of the Church of the Nativity leads into the courtyard of the Greek Orthodox monastery. On the left is the Chapel of St George (12th c.). On the E side is the lower part of the 12th c. bell-tower.

Chapel of St George

Grotto of the Milk

Not far from the Church of the Nativity is the Grotto of the Milk. Tradition has it that the Holy Family stayed here briefly and that while Mary was suckling the infant Jesus a few drops of her milk fell to the ground and turned the rock into soft white stone. There is thought to have been a church dedicated to St Paula on this spot in the 5th c. The grotto was acquired by the Franciscans in c. 1350. The present buildings date from 1872. Some fragments of masonry have been preserved from the earlier buildings.
Mostly women come to pray in the grotto chapel and some of them, having said a prayer, take a piece of the white stone and grind it into a fine powder. Mixed with water to form a drink this is supposed to given them enough milk to feed their babies.

Beit Sahur (Village of the Shepherds)

Beit Sahur, the Village of the Shepherds, lies about 0·62 mile/ 1 km E of Bethlehem. Its people are mostly Christians. It has several churches and various religious institutes. The Franciscan church, which was completely renovated in 1954, is particularly interesting.

Among the fertile fields behind Beit Sahur is the one known as the Field of Ruth. This is supposed to be the scene of the Old Testament idyll described in the Book of Ruth where the poor but beauteous Ruth was gleaning in the field belonging to Boaz who saw her there and straightway fell in love with her. Traditionally these fields were also the place where the shepherds received the tidings of the birth of Christ: "For unto you is born this day in the city of David (=Bethlehem) a Saviour, which is Christ the Lord" (Luke 2:11).

Ruth's Field

E of Beit Sahur is the Greek Orthodox Monastery of the Shepherds. One of the numerous grottos is said to be where the shepherds lived. Excavations have revealed grottos, cisterns and grain stores. Steps in the large walled square lead to an early-Christian chapel.

Monastery of the Shepherds

Rachel's Tomb: a Jewish shrine in an Arab district

Tomb of Rachel

1¼ miles/2 km N of Bethlehem is the Tomb of Rachel. Genesis relates that Rachel, the wife of Jacob, died when giving birth to Benjamin and "was buried in the way to Ephrat, which is Bethlehem" (35:19; 48:7).

The present domed building dates mainly from the 18th to 19th c. In 1841 the little anteroom containing the Mihrab, the Moslem prayer niche, was added. It was thoroughly restored in 1967.

Bethphage

See Mount of Olives

Chief Rabbinate (Hakhal Shlomo)   E6

Location
Ha-Melekh George

Buses
4, 7, 8, 9, 10, 17

Opening times
Sun.–Thurs. 9 a.m.–1 p.m.,
Fri. 9 a.m.–noon.

The Hakhal Shlomo is the seat of the Israeli Chief Rabbinate, the highest court dealing with matters of religion. The building houses a museum of Jewish ritual objects and an Italian synagogue. To the east of Hakhal Shlomo stands the new central synagogue (1982).

Free tours take place from Sun. to Fri. between 9 a.m. and noon.

Church of the Dormition

See Mount Zion

* * Church of the Holy Sepulchre   E7/8

The Church of the Holy Sepulchre, which also contains the last Stations of the Via Dolorosa (see entry), incorporates the sites of Christ's Crucifixion, Entombment and Resurrection. Each chapel and section of the interior commemorates an event associated with Christ's Passion or Resurrection.

Yet although the Church of the Holy Sepulchre is one of the holiest sites in Christendom it does not tower majestically over its surroundings but is cramped into a huddle of shops and houses, has chapels, cells and monasteries added on to it in all directions, and looks like a jumbled and labyrinthine heap of the most disparate component parts.

Six Christian communities (Greek Orthodox, Roman Catholic, Armenians, Syrians, Copts and Abyssinians) are responsible for this church, which means that each jealously guards its own territory and is always on the lookout to catch one of the others in the act of violating the status quo.

No lamp, no picture, nothing whatsoever may be moved without its giving rise to a complaint. The rules governing when and where each community may celebrate Mass are minutely prescribed, as are the times when the lamps may be lit and the windows may be opened. Everything must be done in accordance with the originally agreed rules, i.e. the "status quo" which was set down in writing in 1852. Modifications to this are persistently being sought and just as persistently rejected – they even cropped up in the negotiations for the Treaty of Versailles and in the League of Nations.

This status quo accords the Greek Orthodox community the most rights, and they exercise the largest share (65%) of control over the Church of the Holy Sepulchre. Then come the Roman Catholics, known here as "Latins", and the Armenians; the Copts and the Syrians have only one chapel each. The Ethiopian Abyssinians are the real outsiders, with only the Tomb of Joseph of Arimathea to call their own (a tiny cavity that can only be reached by passing through Coptic territory), and they are housed like outcasts in minute cells on the church roof under Jerusalem's broiling sun.

Near the Abyssinians the Copts also have a rooftop monastery. They occasionally show their contempt for the luckless Abyssinians by quarrelling with them, a situation which erupted into rioting and general mayhem when they disrupted the Abyssinians' Easter celebrations in 1967.

Anyone hoping to find harmony and quiet contemplation reigning among the Christian communities in the Church of the Holy Sepulchre is due for a disappointment – the sects are on a Cold War footing. Even the background noise can be put down to psychological warfare – the sound of the blows of hammers and chisels constantly engaged on improvement work mingles with the chanting of Greek plainsong, blasts from the Franciscan organ and the continual tinkling of Armenian bells.

Location
Old Town

Buses
1, 19, 20, 23

Opening times
Summer: 4 a.m.–8 p.m.
Winter: 4 a.m.–7 p.m.

Status quo

51

Ornamentation at the entrance to the Church of the Holy Sepulchre

There have, however, also been signs of interdenominational concord. In 1958, after 30 years of negotiations, an agreement was finally reached on the carrying out of repairs. And in 1964 Pope Paul VI was allowed to say Mass at a time over which the Roman Catholics had no rights whatever.

Despite all this (or perhaps for this very reason) a visit to the Church of the Holy Sepulchre is quite an experience.

History

When Helena, the mother of Emperor Constantine the Great, visited Jerusalem in 326 Bishop Makarios informed her that the Crucifixion sites and Christ's Tomb were located underneath the temple to Venus built by Emperor Hadrian in A.D. 135. At Helena's urging, Constantine had these sites thoroughly investigated and when this met with success he had the temple to Venus demolished. In 326 he ordered a start to be made on the construction of a basilica over the holy places which was finally consecrated in 335.

After its destruction by the Persians in 614 Abbot Modestus had the church rebuilt in 629. The Moslem desert horsemen led by Caliph Omar inflicted no damage on the church in 638 but in 1009 it was systematically destroyed by the Fatimid Caliph El Hakim.

When he became emperor in 1042 Constantine Monomachos undertook to pay for its reconstruction but lack of money ruled out the rebuilding of Constantine's basilica. Only the rotunda above Christ's Tomb was identical with the 4th c. church. Between 1099 and 1149 the Crusaders added a Romanesque church on to the rotunda.

Despite the disastrous fire of 1808, which resulted in what was in part a rather tasteless rebuilding, and despite the severe earthquake in 1927, the present-day Church of the Holy Sepulchre is basically identical to the Crusader building consecrated in 1149.

Visitors to the Church of the Holy Sepulchre must be suitably dressed (e.g. no short trousers or short-sleeved shirts and blouses).

A portico leads into the atrium which serves as the place where the street meets the shrine and should be viewed as such. This is where the Romanesque façade of the Crusader building soars heavenwards, and at no other point in the church is there such a feeling of tranquil grandeur.

Façade

Fragments of Roman columns are scattered about the square.

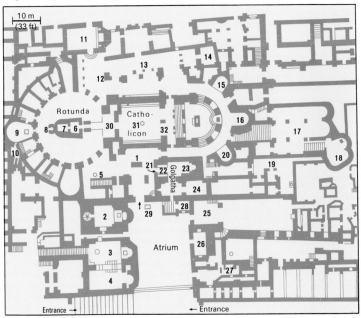

Church of the Holy Sepulchre

1 Stone of Unction
2 Chapel of Forty Martyrs and Belfry
3 Chapel of St John and Baptistry
4 Chapel of St James
5 Stone of the Three Women (Armenian Orthodox)
6 Chapel of the Angel
7 Holy Tomb
8 Chapel of the Copts
9 Chapel of the Jacobites (Syrian Orthodox)

10 Tomb of Joseph of Arimathea (Abyssinian)
11 Franciscan Chapel (Catholic)
12 Mary Magdelene Altar (Catholic)
13 Archway of the Virgin
14 Christ's Prison (chapel; Greek Orthodox)
15 St Longin's Chapel (Greek Orthodox)
16 Chapel of the Sharing of the Raiment (Armenian Orthodox)
17 St Helena's Chapel (Armenian Orthodox)
18 Crypt of the Finding of the Cross (Catholic)
19 Medieval Cloister
20 Chapel of the Insults

21 Chapel of Adam (Greek Orthodox)
22 Site of tombs of Godefroy de Bouillon and Baldwin I
23 Cruxifixion Altar and Stabat Mater Altar (Greek Orthodox)
24 Chapel of the Crucifixion (Catholic)
25 Chapel of St Michael
26 Chapel of St John (Armenian)
27 Abraham's Chapel
28 Chapel of the Sorrows (Mary the Egyptian)
29 Tomb of Philippe d'Aubigny
30 Latin Choir (Catholic)
31 Navel of the World (omphalos)
32 Greek Choir

53

First on the right comes the Greek Orthodox Monastery of Abraham while Greek Orthodox, Armenian and Coptic chapels line the rest of the courtyard.

The steps to the right of the church portal were used by the Crusaders to gain access to Golgotha but this entrance was blocked up in the 12th c.

At the entrance to the Church of the Holy Sepulchre there are two richly decorated portals. The original lintels are in the Rockefeller Museum (see entry). The Raising of Lazarus, the Entry into Jerusalem and the Last Supper can be seen above the right-hand portal while the lintel of the left-hand portal principally contains plant motifs.

A ladder on the church roof is worth mentioning because it appears in sketches and paintings as early as the 19th c. No one removes it, nobody knows why it is there and apparently it is outlasting even the restoration work as a typical by-product of the "status quo"; no change means no contretemps. The Moslem doorkeepers at the church entrance are descendants of the two families that have kept the keys and watched over the church since the Ottoman period.

Interior

The first thing the visitor notices on entering the surprisingly light interior of the church is the Stone of Unction.

Stone of Unction

The Stone of Unction, a red limestone slab with the lamps of the various communities overhead, is owned in common by all the sects represented in the church. This stone is first mentioned during the Crusades but its setting dates from 1810.

This is where, according to the Greek tradition, the body of Christ was removed from the Cross and where, according to the

The Stone of Unction in the Church of the Holy Sepulchre

The Rotunda in the Church of the Holy Sepulchre

Catholic belief, it was anointed before being entombed. The act of Unction, or anointment, was a mark of respect to the dead man and should not be confused with embalming.

The following passage from the Gospel of St John shows that the holy places were very close together: "And after this Joseph of Arimathaea, being a disciple of Jesus, but secretly for fear of the Jews, besought Pilate that he might take away the body of Jesus: and Pilate gave him leave. He came therefore, and took the body of Jesus. And there came also Nicodemus, which at the first came to Jesus by night, and brought a mixture of Myrrh and aloes, about an hundred pound weight. Then took they the body of Jesus, and wound it in linen clothes with the spices, as the manner of the Jews is to bury. Now in the place where he was crucified there was a garden; and in the garden a new sepulchre, wherein was never man yet laid. There laid they Jesus therefore because of the Jews' preparation day; for the sepulchre was nigh at hand." (John 19:38 et seq.)

The wall behind the Stone of Unction is decorated with Greek Orthodox icons.

Further to the left is the "Place of the Three Women" or 'Place of the Three Marys", a stone slab which belongs to the Armenians. The Three Marys were Mary the mother of Jesus, her sister of the same name and Mary Magdalene. According to John 19:25 these three women stood by the Cross.

Past the "Place of the Three Women" one comes to the Rotunda.

Place of the Three Women

The Rotunda is the only part of the present Church of the Holy Sepulchre that still conforms with the "Anastasis", Emperor

Rotunda

55

Constantine's "Church of the Resurrection". It has the same shape and the outer walls date from Constantine up to a height of 36 ft/11 m.

Marble columns and 18 huge pillars support the dome, a wooden construction dating from 1810, reinforced with iron in 1868.

The ambulatory has become a mixture of chapels, storerooms and living quarters for the various communities. Like the Stone of Unction, the Rotunda is the common property of all the communities represented in the Church of the Holy Sepulchre (but this is as far as the community spirit goes).

Holy Sepulchre

In the centre of the Rotunda stands the Holy Sepulchre. The Rococo "pavilion" above it was not built until after the disastrous fire of 1808. It belongs to the Greek Orthodox and the Armenians. The original rock tomb was demolished in 1009 on the orders of Caliph El Hakim.

The Sepulchre is 27·4 ft/8·3 m long and 19·4 ft/5·9 m in width and height. There are 16 columns along the side walls but the most striking decorative feature consists of the lamps presented by popes, emperors, kings and other potentates wishing to influence the status quo. There are 43 of them; the Greeks, Latins and Armenians each having 13 and 4 belonging to the Copts.

The rock under the Tomb has for centuries been thought to be the chamber where Christ was entombed, an assumption that has largely been substantiated by research and archaeological investigations. In the 19th c., however, General Gordon discovered the "Garden Tomb" (see entry) which is still regarded by some Anglicans as the true tomb of Christ.

According to the Gospels of St John and St Mathew Christ's Tomb was very close to the site of the Crucifixion and belonged to Joseph of Arimathea. After the Entombment a rock was rolled over the entrance.

Chapel of the Angels

The visitor first enters an anteroom (11 ft/3·4 m wide and 12·8 ft/3·9 m long), the "Chapel of the Angel". Here can be seen a stone on which the angel sat when he told the women of Christ's Resurrection.

"In the end of the sabbath, as it began to dawn toward the first day of the week, came Mary Magdalene and the other Mary (the mother of James the Younger) to see the sepulchre. And, behold, there was a great earthquake: for the angel of the Lord descended from heaven, and came and rolled back the stone from the door, and sat upon it . . . And the angel answered and said unto the women, Fear not ye: for I know that ye seek Jesus, which was crucified. He is not here: for he is risen, as he said." (Matthew 28:1 et seq.)

Tomb

From the Chapel of the Angel a narrow passage leads to the marble-lined sepulchral chamber. This is also the last Station of the Via Dolorosa (see entry). Christ's resting place was under the slab of reddish-yellow marble on the right-hand wall.

Advice

The chamber is very small with room for only four people at a time. This can lead to crowding and queueing so visitors are requested not to stay more than a few minutes.

Easter celebrations

At Easter the various religious communities hold celebrations in the Rotunda and in front of the Holy Sepulchre. Since the sects hold differing views on the exact timing of the Resurrection not all the celebrations are held on the same day.

The most spectacular event is the appearance of the "holy fire". The entrance to the Chapel of the Angel is sealed on Good Friday then on Easter Saturday the Greek Orthodox patriarch, having removed his crown and vestments, enters the Holy Tomb accompanied by an Armenian priest. The door is locked behind them again and in the Rotunda a great mass of people, holding candles, torches and lanterns, await the appearance of the holy fire. As soon as smoke drifts through an opening in the side wall of the Tomb the crowd erupts into rejoicing at the "miracle": the Archangel Gabriel has presented the Patriarch with Heaven's light.

The Patriarch leaves the Tomb with the holy fire, and the faithful try to light their candles, lamps and torches from the spill the Patriarch holds in his hand. In 1834 people were trampled underfoot in the rush. There are also tales of people becoming transfixed with wonder and screaming with ecstasy, as they dance, howl, pray, swing their torches, tear off their clothes in the frenzy of a "heathen" trance, hug one another and hurl their bodies into the air.

At the rear of the Holy Sepulchre is the Chapel of the Copts where, at the base of the altar, one can see a part of the rock tomb.

Chapel of the Copts

Opposite the Chapel of the Copts, between two pillars, is the Chapel of the Syrian Jacobites. Constantine's 4th c. wall can be seen here.

Chapel of the Jacobites

A low narrow door behind the Chapel of the Jacobites leads into the Abyssinians' "Tomb of Joseph of Arimathea", a 1st c. A.D. Jewish burial chamber.

Tomb of Joseph of Arimathea

According to the Gospel of Nicodemus, Joseph of Arimathea was shut up in a sealed chamber by the Jews because he had asked Pilate for the body of Christ (see above, Stone of Unction). During the night of the Resurrection Christ rescued him from the chamber without breaking the seal.

According to the historian Josephus Flavius, however, when Jerusalem was taken by Titus in A.D. 70 a thick wall was breached to reveal, on the other side, a venerable old man with snow-white hair who declared himself to be Joseph of Arimathea. He said he had been walled up by the Jews (a second time?) because he had buried Christ. Celestial food and celestial light had kept him alive.

The Altar of Mary Magdalene is reached by passing between two columns on the N side of the Rotunda. Closer inspection of the tapering of these columns reveals that they are the top half and the bottom half of a single column.

Altar of Mary Magdalene

The Roman Catholics' Altar of Mary Magdalene commemorates Jesus' appearance to Mary Magdalene while the women were standing in bewilderment in front of the empty Tomb. At first Mary Magdalene thought that the man who had suddenly appeared was the gardener and suspected him of having removed Jesus' body. But the man she supposed to be the gardener was the Risen Christ. He told her to go forth and tell others that she had seen the Lord (John 20:14 et seq.).

To the N of this altar are the sacristy and other rooms belonging to the Franciscans where there is an organ.

Chapel of Adam

The Holy Sepulchre

E of the Altar of Mary Magdalene is the "Archway of the Virgin", an arcade of seven arches with different columns (probably 11th c.).

Archway of the Virgin

At the E end of this aisle can be seen a Greek Orthodox chapel known (without any historical foundation) as "Christ's Prison". (The sites of the prison and the Crucifixion were well distant from each other.)

Christ's Prison

In the E ambulatory of the choir is the Chapel of St Longinus. Longinus is identified in the Apocrypha with the Roman soldier who pierced Jesus' side with a spear (John 19:34) or with the Roman centurion who cried out, "Truly this man was the Son of God!", when the veil of the Temple was rent on the death of Jesus (Mark 15:39).

Longinus Chapel

Next to the Longinus Chapel, also in the E ambulatory of the choir, is the Armenian "Chapel of the Sharing of the Raiment". This chapel recalls that after the Crucifixion the soldiers shared out Jesus' garments and cast lots for his seamless body-linen (John 19:23 et seq.).

Chapel of the Sharing of the Raiment

Steps next to the Chapel of the Sharing of the Raiment lead to the Armenian Chapel of Helena. The rock wall on the right is covered with small crosses, most of which were scratched by medieval pilgrims seeking immortality but, unlike today, refraining from indulging in personal graffiti and preferring instead to identify themselves as part of the Christian community.

Chapel of Helena

The 12th c. Crusader chapel has a nave and two aisles, each of which has an apse. Four squat columns support the dome of what is perhaps the most charming and appealing feature in the Church of the Holy Sepulchre as a whole. The massive capitals date back to the 8th c. (Above the roof of the dome, through which the light enters, are the cells of the Ethiopian Abyssinians.)

From the Chapel of Helena 13 narrow steps lead to the sparsely furnished Crypt of the Finding of the Cross, a former cistern. This is where a Jew by the name of Judas, who later became a Christian and died the death of a martyr, is said to have helped the empress to find the True Cross, complete with nails, together with the two thieves' crosses.

Crypt of the Finding of the Cross

On ascending the stairs from the Crypt of the Finding of the Cross and the Chapel of Helena the visitor returns to the E choir ambulatory. On the left at the top of the stairs is the Greek Orthodox "Oratory of the Insults".
The stump of a column on view here is said to be part of the column to which Jesus was bound when he was insulted, beaten and flogged by the Roman soldiers.

Oratory of the Insults

On the right of the E aisle is the entrance to the Catholicon (see below) and straight ahead is the Stone of Unction. Left of the Stone of Unction is the entrance to the Chapel of Adam.

The Greek Orthodox Chapel of Adam, which is richly decorated with icons and reliquaries, is where, according to legend, Adam's skull was discovered at the moment of Christ's crucifixion.

Chapel of Adam

Part of the rock of Golgotha can be seen through a sheet of glass. On the right of the altar a metal rail hides the crack in the rock described in Matthew 27:51: "When Jesus died the earth quaked and the rock split."
On each side of the entrance stone slabs represent the tombs, broken up in 1808, of the first rulers of the Crusader Kingdom, Godefroy de Bouillon (1099–1100) and Baldwin I de Boulogne (1100–18).

Golgotha

On each side of the Chapel of Adam steep stairs lead to Golgotha or Calvary, some 16 ft/5 m above. Here one finds Stations X–XIII of the Via Dolorosa (see entry). To visit them in the right order pilgrims should take the Roman Catholic steps on the right; these lead to the Chapel of Sorrows and the Crucifixion Altar.
In the gospels Golgotha is referred to as "the place of the skull". This corresponds to Calvary, derived from the Latin "calvaria" meaning cranium but the interpretations of the two names are contradictory. Origenes, the Greek writer on church matters, attributes the name to the fact that this is where Adam's skull was found (see above, Chapel of Adam). The most likely explanation is that Golgotha referred to a skull-shaped hill outside the city wall of Jerusalem of that time which also served as a place of judgement and of burial. Jerome, the Latin Father of the Church, on the other hand, derived the name Golgotha from the skulls of those who were buried there.

Altar of the Crucifixion
The Roman Catholic Altar of the Crucifixion is very moving with the unassuming splendour of its reliefs and its realistic mosaics, most of which are illuminated. The Chapel of the Sorrows (previously the Chapel of the Franks) in the immediate vicinity is where the Franciscans celebrate their daily Mass.

Stabat Mater Altar
The Stabat Mater Altar is also Roman Catholic and commemorates the spot where "the sorrowing mother stood" (stabat mater dolorosa) and suffered with her crucified son.

Altar of the Crucifixion
The Greek Orthodox Altar of the Crucifixion is smothered with lamps and icons. Under the altar, inlaid with silver, is the hole in the rock which held Christ's cross. Two dark-coloured discs show where the thieves' crosses stood. In the lunette behind the altar are life-size representations of Mary, Jesus and John, his favourite disciple.

Catholicon

After descending the E stairs, belonging to the Orthodox Greeks and leading to the Altar of the Crucifixion, the visitor finds the Catholicon straight ahead.
The nave of the Crusader church belongs to the Orthodox Greeks who had walls erected all over the place in order to create the Catholicon as a place of their own within the church. Almost all the walls of the Catholicon were improved during the repairs and the pillars have also been partially replaced.
The main feature of the Catholicon is the marble basin under the dome, the "omphalos", which is supposed to represent the "navel" of the world.

View from the Church of the Redeemer over the Old Town ▶

Church of Mary Magdalene

See Mount of Olives

Church of the Nations

See Mount of Olives

Church of the Nativity

See Bethlehem

Church of the Redeemer   E8

Location
Bet ha Bad (Old Town)

Buses
1, 12, 27

Opening times
Mon. 9 a.m.–1 p.m.,
Tues.–Sat. 9 a.m.–1 p.m.,
2–5 p.m.

The quarter in which the German Evangelical Lutheran Church of the Redeemer stands is called "Muristan", the Persian word for "hospice". Hospices were lodging houses founded by monks for pilgrims and travellers, mainly in places of pilgrimage. In the 9th c. Charlemagne founded the Latin Quarter in Jerusalem and had a hospice and the Church of Santa Maria Latina built. This is also where the Order of the Knights Hospitallers was founded (later to become the Knights of St John).

In 1869 the whole Muristan district was in ruins (El Hakim had laid waste to it in 1009) when Crown Prince Friedrich Wilhelm of Prussia visited the Holy Land and bought the site. In accordance with the original ground plans the Prussians built the Church of the Redeemer in the 12th c. style over the ruins of the former hospice and the Church of Santa Maria Latina. The building work uncovered fragments of the so-called Second Wall (see Alexandra Hospice). The church was consecrated on the occasion of Kaiser Wilhelm II's visit on 31.12.1898.

The oldest preserved sections are the medieval gate with the signs of the zodiac and the symbols of the months, and parts of the cloister.

From the tower there is a magnificent view over the whole of the Old Town as far as the Mount of Olives and Mount Zion (see entries).

The Greek Orthodox obtained the W part of the site and built the Church of St Abraham and a monastery. In the SW corner of the Muristan is a church dedicated to St John the Baptist.

Citadel with David's Tower   E7

Location
Jaffa Gate

Buses
1, 19, 20, 23

Opening times
Sept.–May: daily, 8.30 a.m.–
4.30 p.m.; June–Aug.: daily,
8.30 a.m.–7 p.m.; Fri. only
until 2 p.m.

To the right of the Jaffa Gate (see entry) stands the citadel on the site of the palace of Herod the Great; its Tower of David can be seen from a distance. One of the buildings in the citadel now houses a museum.

Today the citadel includes five towers: the E Tower near the entrance, the SE and the NW towers (opposite Jaffa Gate), David's Tower and the Tower of the Mosque. The NW Tower and the Tower of the Mosque have openings in the outer walls from which attackers could be repulsed.

The citadel: on the site of Herod's Palace ▶

The citadel used to be entirely surrounded by a ditch but in 1898 this was largely filled in so that Wilhelm II, the German kaiser, could make his entrance into the Old Town by coach (parts of the Old Town Wall between the Jaffa Gate and the citadel were pulled down to accommodate this procession).

Herod's Palace
The citadel occupies the ground where once the palace of Herod the Great stood; this was erected in 24 B.C., and some remains still exist. Excavations have also uncovered parts of foundations dated to the pre-Herodian, Hashmonean period. It is possible that the palace of the Hashmonean kings also stood here.

Large parts of the Phasael Tower remains, named after Herod's brother who was murdered during the conquest of Jerusalem because of the Antigonos rebellion. The huge smooth blocks present an impressive picture of the quality and solidity of Herodian building methods.

The other two towers protecting Herod's palace were named after his friend Hippikus and his wife Mariamne.

After A.D. 6 the praetorium of the Roman governor was probably sited here. In A.D. 66 the palace was burnt down by Jewish resistance fighters. Following the conquest of Jerusalem in A.D. 70 Titus decided against destroying the towers (because of their solid construction it would have been too expensive to pull them down). He proclaimed the towers to be "symbols of the bravery of Roman soldiers" and assigned them to the X Legio Fratensis as quarters. The sign of the legion, XLF, is to be seen on many columns, stones, tiles and pipes.

Later Buildings
The Moslem administration later made this its headquarters and there was a Crusader fortress here which was destroyed in 1239. In 1335 the Mamelukes rebuilt the citadel and built a minaret on David's Tower. The name "David's Tower" is erroneous: it was thought that this was Mount Zion, David's City.

The present form of the citadel was, to a large extent, the work of Sultan Suleiman the Magnificent who erected the wall around the Old Town between 1537 and 1540.

Museum

The citadel houses the city's historical museum. Exhibits document the history of the area of the citadel from Hashmonean times up to the 20th c. Very good guided tours in English take place on weekdays at 8.30 and 10.30 a.m., 12.30, 2.30 and 6.30 p.m.; the last tour on Fri. at 12.30 p.m.

Son et Lumière

Every evening from April to October (except Fridays and the evenings before public holidays) there is a "son et lumière" show called: "A stone in David's Tower".

The English programme starts at 8.45 p.m. and the French version (which is only on Sundays and Thursdays) at 10 p.m. On Monday, Tuesday, Wednesday and Saturday entertainments in the English language are also provided in the courtyard of the citadel (warm clothing is recommended).

Coenaculum (Room of the Last Supper)

See Mount Zion

Damascus Gate: magnificent guardian of the city

*Damascus Gate

D8

The monumental Damascus Gate is the main access to the Old Town from northern modern Jerusalem. It is on the dividing line between the Christian and Moslem quarters and is the finest of the seven open Old Town gates.

Each of the religious communities has a different name for this gate. The Jews call it "Sichem Gate" (Sha'ar Shekhem), because from it the Derekh Shekhem leads to Sichem (see Nablus); the Christians use its official title, the Damascus Gate, and the Moslems call it the "Gate of the Pillar" (Bab el-Amud) because of the pillar from which the distance to Damascus is measured.

Of the six gates built by Sultan Suleiman the Magnificent in 1537–40 as entrances through the walls, only the Jaffa, Zion (see entries) and Damascus gates survive in their original form. At almost 46 ft/14 m high the Damascus Gate is the largest and most massive, and serves as an outstanding example of Ottoman defensive architecture.

Entry is through a corridor full of corners to slow down any attackers. The broad façade of the gate is flanked by two huge towers so that any enemy was open to attack on three sides. Besides engaging the enemy from the platforms on the top of the walls, the defenders could fire at them from the floors inside the gate itself through the slits that reveal the position of these floors in the interior. Projecting from the tower corners nearest the gate are the bays of the guardrooms.

The Arabic inscription on the lintel below the arch states that

Location
Corner of Sultan Suleiman/ Derekh Shekhem

Buses
12, 27

Opening times
Wall: Sat.–Thurs. 9 a.m.– 5 p.m., Fri. 9 a.m.–3 p.m.

65

walls and gates were built on the orders of Suleiman the Magnificent.

Below the bridge can be seen remains of the so-called Third Wall that was completed only shortly before Jerusalem was destroyed by Titus (A.D. 70) although it had been begun by Herod Agrippa I in A.D. 40. The small gate also belongs to this Third Wall. It is one of the two passageways for pedestrians that flanked a large gate for vehicles (renovated by Emperor Hadrian in A.D. 135).

The pillar to which the gate owes its Moslem name is on the far side of the gate. This column is said to date from the time of Emperor Hadrian who built the Roman city Aelia Capitolina in A.D. 135 on the ruins of what had been Jerusalem. There is, however, no historical mention of the column until the 6th c., when it was recorded on the "Map of Madaba", a large mosaic pavement (538 sq. ft/50 sq. m) in the Greek Orthodox church of Madaba (Jordan), the oldest geographical representation of Palestine and the Nile Delta.

The "cardo maximus" (N–S axis) of Hadrian's Aelia Capitolina left the city by the Damascus Gate and this street still follows the same course today.

---

*Dead Sea

Location
28 miles/45 km SE

At 1069 ft/392 m below sea level, the Dead Sea is the lowest point on the earth's surface. Its salt content is almost nine times as great as that of the Mediterranean. The density of water allows one to lie motionless on the surface without sinking. It is possible to take a meal on a tray into the water with you and so enjoy both the meal and the healing effects of the water simultaneously. Most of the bathing places are found in the SW of this salty lake where a health resort has become established. The water does have healing effects (e.g. blood pressure) but if it gets into the lungs, it can be fatal. For the name "Dead Sea" is a euphemism: the Dead Sea is not dead, it kills. No fish, no living thing (excepting microscopic organisms such as sulphur bacteria) can survive in this water. It used to be thought that a bird could not even fly over the Dead Sea. Bitumen was obtained here in antiquity. Today one can see the evaporation plants for potash, bromine and magnesium salts.

Qumran

On the W bank of the Dead Sea lie the ruins of Qumran, the famous settlement of the Jewish sect of the Essene (="the pious ones").

About the mid 2nd c. B.C. under Herod the Great, a fortified monastery was established here on the foundations of a building dating from the 9th to 6th c. B.C. It was then deserted and later resettled. Most of the monks, however, lived in caves outside the cloisters. The majority of the community's members had chosen to opt out of civilisation.

The Essene rejected the Jewish rite of sacrifice, followed the laws of purity and lived here in a community of monks. Before the Romans destroyed their settlement in A.D. 68, the monks hid their scrolls in the numerous caves. In 1947 two Bedouin shepherds found a scroll several metres long bearing the text of the book of Isaiah. This scroll and other Essene manuscripts are now on display in the "Shrine of the Book" in the Israel Museum (see entry).

Qumran on the Dead Sea: refuge of the Essene 2000 years ago

Dome of the Rock

See Haram esh-Sharif

Dominus Flevit (Church)

See Mount of Olives

Dung Gate
E8

The Dung Gate in the S wall is the smallest of the Old Town gates and recent alterations have made it the ugliest. Its name comes from the fact that this was where the dung was taken out of the town. Ancient Jerusalem had its rubbish dump outside the Dung Gate, the name by which it was already known in the Old Testament (Nehemiah 2:13; 3:13–14; 12:31).

As with all the gates built by Suleiman the Magnificent when he erected the city wall in 1537–40, the passage through the Dung Gate was also full of corners to make defence easier (see Damascus Gate). The Jordanians straightened this crooked passage so that motor traffic could pass through. They also enlarged the gateway, but the small arch above the new lintel shows just how small it was originally.

The Arabic name is Bab el Magharbeh (Gate of the Moors), since this was where the North Africans who had been recruited by Suleiman lived after their work of building the wall had been completed.

Location
S Old Town

Opening times
Wall: Sat.–Thurs. 9 a.m.–7 p.m., Fri. 9 a.m.–3 p.m.

67

Ecce Homo Arch

See Via Dolorosa

Ecole Biblique et Archéologique Française

See St Stephen

El Aqsa Mosque

See Haram esh-Sharif

Elijah Monastery (Deir Mar Elias)

Location
Mar Elias, 5 miles/8 km S

Bus
22 (from the Damascus Gate)

Taxis
From the Damascus and Jaffa gates

The Greek Orthodox Elijah Monastery is situated on a hill on the road from Jerusalem to Bethlehem (see entry). The fortress-like building was constructed in 1160 on the foundations of an earlier demolished 5th c. monastery. It was altered and renovated in the 17th c.

According to tradition the monastery stands on the site of a hiding place used by the prophet Elijah on his eventful flight from the vengeance of Queen Jezebel after he had opposed the cult of Baal under King Ahab of Israel (871–852 B.C.). After his successful confrontation with the priests of Baal on Mount Carmel Elijah had them all slain but then had to flee from Jezebel, the wife of Ahab (1 Kings 18–19).

The Elijah Monastery: a fortress in the desert

El Qubeiba

El Qubeiba is not only known for its magnificent panoramic view of the surrounding countryside but it is also one of the seven places (cf. entry for Abu Gosh) that lay claim to being the site of Emmaus which, according to Luke's gospel (Luke 24:13), was 60 furlongs from Jerusalem.

On the N side of the medieval road running through El Quebeiba can be seen the excavations of a Crusader village. Also of interest to visitors is the early 20th c. Franciscan church built on the foundations of a 12th c. predecessor. This church contains masonry from a house dating from early Byzantine times. It is thought to be the house of Cleopas, one of the two Disciples whom Jesus met on the road from Jerusalem to Emmaus after the Resurrection, and with whom he ate and broke bread before vanishing from their sight (Luke 24:13 et seq.).

Bus
From the Damascus Gate

Location
8 miles/12 km NW

---

*En Karem (En Kerem)

The village of En Karem, the traditional birthplace of John the Baptist, lies in picturesque countryside on the slope of a hill on the W outskirts of Jerusalem.

John the Baptist's parents were the aged priest Zacharias and his equally elderly wife Elizabeth, a relative of the Virgin Mary. After the Archangel Gabriel had visited Mary and told her of the birth of Jesus, Mary visited Elizabeth "in the hill country in a city of Juda" (Luke 1:39) where she stayed about three months (1:56). The Archangel Gabriel had also promised Zacharias he would be the father of John the Baptist (1:11 et seq.).

In recent years the beauty of the surrounding countryside has attracted many painters and artists to En Karem and it has become a flourishing artists' colony with galleries and restaurants.

En means "spring" and Karem means "vineyard" which, since En Karem has both, is a factual description of the place.

What does not fit the facts, however, is the equating of En Karem with Beth-Charem of the Old Testament. The name Beth-Charem also refers to a vineyard ("vineyard house"), and Beth-Charem was presumably on a hill, since signals could be sent from it (Jeremiah 6:1), but Jeremiah also says that Beth-Charem was to the N of Jerusalem, whereas En Karen lies to the W.

Buses
17

Location
2½ miles/4 km W

St John the Baptist (church)

The Franciscan church of St John the Baptist was built in 1674 on the ruins of a Crusader building but as early as the 5th c. there was a basilica on this spot which was reputed to be John's birthplace.

Six rectangular pillars separate the two aisles from the nave. The high altar is dedicated to John the Baptist and the altar in the right aisle to his mother, St Elizabeth. Especially interesting is the painting of "John in the Wilderness" above the door leading to the sacristy, a 17th or 18th c. copy of a Murillo.

Behind a grille in the right aisle is a piece of rock. According to legend, when (Moslem!) workmen took for lime-burning a piece of the rock venerated as St John's rock standing halfway between En Karem and the desert, the furnace exploded. The crestfallen lime-burners brought a fragment of the rock to the church.

Steps in the left aisle lead to the Grotto of the Nativity. It is quite possible that a grotto of this kind had been the property of the priest Zacharias.

Marble reliefs on the altar depict scenes from the life of John the Baptist.

Grotto of the Nativity

When the present church portal was built in 1885 a 5th c. chapel with two rock-hewn tombs was discovered. A fragment of mosaic has survived with peacocks, partridges and flowers, as well as an inscription in Greek "Hail, Martyr of God".

N chapel

Excavations in 1942 revealed another chapel. The floor of this 5th c. building, with a nave, two aisles and an apse at the E end, is decorated with mosaics. Steps lead into a grotto where vases dating from the time of Herod were found.

S chapel

The excavations in 1942 also produced the so-called Venus Pudica, the "Coy Venus".

Spring of the Virgin

Between the Church of St John the Baptist and the Church of the Visitatio Mariae is the Spring of the Virgin. It rises in a cave in the rock (around which stands an abandoned mosque) and since the 14th c. has been associated with the Virgin Mary who is said to have drawn water from it.

Visitatio Mariae (Church)

The Church of the Visitatio Mariae, dedicated to the visit Mary paid to her relative Elizabeth, consists of the modern upper church (1955) and the somewhat older lower church.

Although the Franciscans bought the site – with a dilapidated Crusader building over the so-called house of St Elizabeth – as early as 1679, it was another 200 years before they got permission from the Moslems to build the present lower church.

Both churches have predominantly modern furnishings (impressive frescoes, mosaics). The mosaic on the façade of the upper church depicts Mary's arrival at the home of Elizabeth. The pilasters are decorated with lines from the Magnificat (Luke 1:46 et seq.).

Russian Laura (Convent)

Not far from the Visitatio Mariae church are the buildings of the Russian convent Mar Zakariya. Of particular interest here are the two churches and the so-called Pulpit of John the Baptist. The dwellings of the Russian nuns are in a grove of cypresses.

◀ *The Franciscan church in the artists' colony of En Karem*

St John in the Wilderness

St John in the Wilderness (Franciscan monastery)

In the valley about $1\frac{1}{4}$ miles/2 km from En Karem stands the Franciscan monastery of St John in the Wilderness. The grotto with the "hermit spring", now a chapel, is where St John prepared in solitude to go forth and baptize (Luke 1:80).
The monastery and the church were built in 1922, but there are traces of monastery buildings dating from the 12th c.

*Garden Tomb   D8

Location
Derekh Shekhem

Buses
12, 27

Opening times
Mon.–Sat. 8 a.m.–
12.30 p.m., 3–5 or 5.30 p.m.

The "Garden Tomb" is a tomb with two chambers cut out of the rock, and dates from the time of Christ. It is in a beautifully laid-out garden on the Derekh Shekhem not far from the Damascus Gate (see entry). Many Anglicans believe it to be the true tomb of Christ.

The "proofs" advanced by General Gordon, who discovered this tomb on a visit to Jerusalem in 1883, are a hotchpotch of fanciful mysticism and dubious arguments. He looked upon the whole of Jerusalem as a skeleton with the Temple Mount (see Haram esh-Sharif) as its pelvis, Solomon's Quarries (see Zedekiah's Cave) as its ribs, and the Garden Tomb site its skull. In this Gordon was basing his ideas on the reports of the Evangelists that Jesus was crucified and buried on Golgotha. Golgotha means "place of the skull" and this was assumed to mean a skull-shaped hill. This hill must, however, have been outside the city walls of that time since burial places were

"Garden Tomb": a quiet resting place, however unauthentic

considered unclean and were not allowed inside the city walls.
The Garden Tomb is in fact outside the present city walls but
these do not follow the same line as the city wall in Jesus' time.
And the Tomb of Joseph of Arimathea, an ancient Jewish
burial chamber of the 1st c. A.D. in the Church of the Holy
Sepulchre (see entry), is clear testimony to the fact that there
was a burial place on the spot where the church now stands in
the time of Jesus. Cf. also Alexandra Hospice (see entry).

The arguments for and against the Garden Tomb have,
however, resulted in the English society founded by General
Gordon tidying up this spot and laying out a very beautiful
garden with arbours and seating. Although the Garden Tomb,
or "Gordon's Tomb" as it is also known, continues to be a holy
place for many Anglicans, it has none of the hurly-burly found
at the Church of the Holy Sepulchre and lends itself much more
to quiet contemplation.

Gethsemane

See Mount of Olives

Gihon Spring

See Kidron Valley

Golden Gate

See Harem esh-Sharif

Grotto of the Milk

See Bethlehem

Hadassah Hospital

See Mount Scopus

*Hadassah Medical Centre (University Hospital)

Location
Kirjat Hadassah

Buses
19, 27

When in 1948 it became no longer possible to use the Hadassah Hospital on Mount Scopus (see entry), the Zionist Hadassah Women's Organisation of America founded this huge building complex above the village of En Karem which, with its hospital and study centre, was completed in 1951.

Synagogue

Opening times
Sun.–Thurs. 2–4 p.m.

The most interesting section of the Hadassah Medical Centre is its Synagogue with the 12 famous windows by Marc Chagall representing scenes from the story of the 12 sons of Jacob.

Guided tours

There are free guided tours generally in English, taking in Chagall's windows and the film "The Hadassah Story", from Sunday to Thursday at 9.30, 10.30, 11.30 a.m. and 12.30 p.m.; last tour on Friday at 11.30 a.m. (assembly point: Kennedy Building). The Friday tours must be booked in advance by telephone (416333). There are no guided tours on Saturdays and public holidays.

Hakel Dama

See Kidron Valley

**Haram esh-Sharif (Temple Mount)

Location
E Old Town

Opening times
Sat.–Thurs. 8 a.m.–sunset

The Moslem name for the Temple precinct on Mount Moriah is Haram esh-Sharif, "the noble sanctuary", or Har Habajit, "the raised shrine". This trapezoidal area, with sides of 532 yd/486 m (W), 489 yd/447 m (E), 347 yd/317 m (N) and 310 yd/283 m (S), covers a sixth of the total area of the Old Town. In the N it is bordered by the Bezetha Valley, in the E by the Kidron Valley (see entry), in the W by the Tyropeion Valley, and in the S by Mount Ophel. It is the site of such highly significant monuments as the Dome of the Rock, the El Aqsa Mosque and the Golden Gate.

In 638 Caliph Omar conquered Jerusalem and declared this site a sacred precinct of Islam. However, temples had stood here 1500 years earlier. The explanation for this lies in the exposed nature of the site: from ancient times the favoured location for Jewish shrines had always been on hilltops and in groves (Mount Moriah="Mount of Olive Trees").

Hadassah Medical Centre: Chagall's stained-glass windows . . .

. . . with scenes from the story of Jacob's sons

The middle of Haram esh-Sharif is about 13 ft/4 m higher than the level of the surrounding precinct. This marks the location – slightly off-centre – of the "holy rock" which is spanned by the Dome of the Rock. This rock is said to be the one on which Abraham nearly sacrificed his son and from which Mohammed rose on horseback up to heaven. Jews and Christians look upon it as the base of the altar for burnt offerings that stood in the temples of Solomon and Herod.

History of Temple Mount

The history of Temple Mount begins with an event very early on in the Old Testament. God ordered Abraham to sacrifice his son Isaac "on a mountain in the land of Moriah". Just as Abraham was about to plunge the sacrificial knife into his son, his hand was stayed by the angel of the Lord (Genesis 22).
Solomon built his Temple "at Jerusalem in Mount Moriah" (2 Chronicles 3:1). According to Jewish tradition Abraham's and Solomon's mountains are one and the same.
According to the Book of Maccabees Solomon ordered his Temple to be built on Mount Zion. This was the acropolis of the city of the Jebusites (Jerusalem) conquered by David which had its name changed to the "City of David" (2 Samuel 5:7–9). This is where David brought the Ark of the Covenant and lodged it in a tent, thus making it the political and religious centre of the country. When David wanted to build a temple for the Ark the word of God came to him that it would be his son Solomon who would build the Temple (2 Samuel 7; see also Introduction, Famous People: David, Solomon).

Solomon's Temple
Solomon's rule began in 964 B.C. Work on the Temple was begun in the fourth year of his reign and took rather more than seven years.
The Temple made up the N section of a temple and palace complex. The secular buildings (armoury, stoa, throne-room, the king's living quarters, harem, etc.) were grouped around courtyards. The Temple, of natural stone clad with cedarwood, consisted of the anteroom, the tabernacle (with an altar for incense, candlesticks and shewbreads) and the windowless adytum (containing the Ark of the Covenant between two gilded cherubim). Immediately in front of these three rooms were two walled courtyards: the "upper" courtyard which was on a rather higher level (containing the altar on which burnt offerings were made and the "sea of brass" for the priests' ablutions) and the "outer" courtyard accessible to all.
The Temple was repeatedly plundered and finally destroyed. In 587 B.C. Nebuchadnezzar razed Jerusalem, stole the Temple treasure (the Ark of the Covenant is not mentioned as being among the spoils) and carried the people off to captivity in Babylon.

The Temple of Zerubbavel
After the conquest of the New Babylonian Kingdom by Cyrus II of Persia (539 B.C.) the Jews recovered the items stolen from the Temple by Nebuchadnezzar, were allowed to return from exile and got permission to build a house of God in Jerusalem. However, construction of the Temple under Zerubbavel, whom Cyrus had appointed governor of Jerusalem, made only slow progress, encumbered by lack of finance and external hostilities and disruption.

The new "Second Temple" was bigger than Solomon's but was nowhere near as magnificent. It lacked the Ark of the Covenant; there was nothing to be seen in the adytum.

During the Hellenisation of Palestine under the Seleucids (from about 198 B.C.) a statue of Zeus was erected on the altar. In 169 B.C. Antiochos IV Epiphanes plundered the Temple which in the interim had become the symbol of Jewish resistance to Seleucid rule.

In 165 B.C. the Maccabees seized Temple Mount and the Temple reverted to its original use (hence the Feast of the Consecration of the Temple).

In 63 B.C. Pompey conquered Jerusalem, forced his way into the (empty) adytum, but did not allow the Temple to be plundered.

In 54 B.C. Crassus Dives plundered the Temple to finance his campaign against the Parthians (dives="rich man").

In 37 B.C. Herod, who had been named King of the Jews by Rome, conquered Jerusalem, and the Temple was once more plundered, desecrated and damaged.

The Temple of Herod the Great

King Herod had to use force to achieve his objectives in Jerusalem, but managed to get the people on his side through his policies which revolved around the demolition and reconstruction of the Temple.

Although Herod pulled down nearly all of Zerubbavel's Temple in order to build his "most magnificent Temple in the world", the Jews made no distinction between Zerubbavel's Temple and that of Herod. The "First" (Solomon's) Temple had been completely destroyed but not the "Second" Temple. Thus although Herod the Great's Temple was in fact the third Temple on Mount Moriah it has entered the history books as the Second Temple.

A great deal of in-filling and piling was required to enable the mighty structure to be built on a flat surface; retaining walls were also built in the E, S and W. Yet, apart from a few fragments, none of Herod's building of that time has survived, although the ground plan of the present Temple precinct corresponds to that of Herod's Temple.

This Temple was surrounded by a strong wall, part of which is still incorporated in the Wailing Wall (see entry). The buildings and the courtyards were larger than those of Solomon's Temple but the proportions were the same. The courtyards in front were terraced one above the other, with the adytum at the top. In the NW of this site with its 13 gates stood the Antonia Fortress (see Via Dolorosa). At each gate was a notice (usually in Latin and Greek) that forbade non-Jews from proceeding any further.

All work on the Temple of Herod the Great was completed in A.D. 65; five years later the Temple was destroyed again.

There is a model of Jerusalem in the garden of the Holyland Hotel (see Practical Information, Hotels) showing the city and the Temple as they were in A.D. 66 (scale 50:1). The historical sources for this monumental model, in addition to the topographical and archaeological research carried out by Professor Avi-Yonah at the Hebrew University, were the Mishnah collections, the Talmud and Josephus Flavius' "Jewish Wars".

N.B.

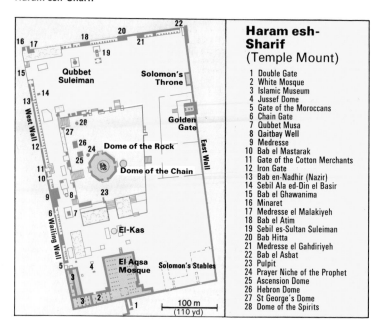

Haram esh-Sharif (Temple Mount)

1 Double Gate
2 White Mosque
3 Islamic Museum
4 Jussef Dome
5 Gate of the Moroccans
6 Chain Gate
7 Qubbet Musa
8 Qaitbay Well
9 Medresse
10 Bab el Mastarak
11 Gate of the Cotton Merchants
12 Iron Gate
13 Bab en-Nadhir (Nazir)
14 Sebil Ala ed-Din el Basir
15 Bab el Ghawanima
16 Minaret
17 Medresse el Malakiyeh
18 Bab el Atim
19 Sebil es-Sultan Suleiman
20 Bab Hitta
21 Medresse el Gahdiriyeh
22 Bab el Asbat
23 Pulpit
24 Prayer Niche of the Prophet
25 Ascension Dome
26 Hebron Dome
27 St George's Dome
28 Dome of the Spirits

The Temple after Herod

Five years after its completion the Second Temple went up in flames when Titus captured Jerusalem. Emperor Hadrian had Jerusalem razed to the ground after putting down the Second Jewish uprising (A.D. 132–135). He constructed the Roman colonial city of Aelia Capitolina where Jerusalem had stood and a temple to Jupiter was built on Mount Moriah (destroyed in 326).

In 361 Emperor Julian Apostata ordered the Temple to be rebuilt but work was suspended after his death (363). The Temple precinct gradually deteriorated into being the town rubbish dump.

Sacred precinct of Islam

Caliph Omar took Jerusalem in 638. Once the square had been cleared of rubbish and debris, he declared it to be the sacred precinct of Islam. This was followed by the building of the El Aqsa Mosque, the Dome of the Rock and other smaller buildings and, despite changing fortunes, the precinct has remained in the hands of the Moslems to this day.

Even the interlude of the Crusades did not bring about any change. From the Temple Mount the Moslems tried to fight off the invading Crusaders (1091) but were soon overcome and horribly slaughtered by those who were supposed to be fighting a Holy War.

The establishment of a Christian kingdom by the Crusaders (1100) was followed by Hughes de Payns founding in 1119 the holy Order of the Knights Templar (Fratres militiae Templi) which took its name from the Temple Mount. This order made itself responsible for protecting the pilgrims to Jerusalem.

With the capture by the Mamelukes of Akkon, the last Crusader fort, the Christian kingdom of Jerusalem came to an end (291), and the Order of Templars was dissolved shortly afterwards on account of heresy and debauchery.

Visiting

The entrances for non-Moslems are on the W side (Old Town side). However, they may only enter through certain gates. These are, from N to S, Bab el Ghawanima, Bab en-Nazir, Bab el Qattanin, Bab es-Silsileh and Bab el Magharibeh. They can leave the precinct by any of the gates.

There are ticket-kiosks for the Dome of the Rock and the El Aqsa Mosque next to Bab en-Nazir and Bab el Magharibeh ("the Gate of the Moors"). Entry to Haram esh-Sharif is free but it is advisable to obtain tickets for the Dome and the Mosque beforehand.

The best way to enter the precinct is by Bab en-Nazir (where there is a kiosk) from Aladdin Road (a turning off Solomon Road).

Although the Dome of the Rock is the central shrine on Haram esh-Sharif the visitor should first inspect the site. Turning right on entering through Bab en-Nazir the visitor passes the "Iron Gate" (Bab el Hadid) and reaches the Qaitbay Well between the stairs leading to the platform and the richly ornamented "Gate of the Cotton Merchants" (Bab el Qattanin; 14th c.).

Qaitbay Well

This strange well was a gift from the Mameluke Sultan Qaitbay and was the work of Egyptian craftsmen in 1487. They seem to have been more familiar with putting up tombs because this is the style in which they built the well. The Jews believe that this was the site of the Temple adytum.

Besides this well there are also a number of cisterns in the square with a total capacity of about 11 million gals./50 million litres. At the time of the Second Temple several of these cisterns were ways into the Temple Mount or passages for priests into the Temple that were later made into cisterns.

Also a gift from Qaitbay and made by Egyptian craftsmen (but not in the form of a tomb this time) is the building that he endowed next to the well (forecourt dilapidated) which projects into the roofed porch of Haram esh-Sharif.

Scales

There are in all eight sets of steps leading up to the 13 ft/4 m high roughly paved platform on which stands the Dome of the Rock. At the top the visitor has to pass through a free-standing arcade.

This arcade is known as "the scales" (mawazin) since Moslems believe that on Judgement Day this is where the scales will be hung in which mankind will be weighed in the balance.

Exterior of the Dome of the Rock: 45,000 faience tiles

** Dome of the Rock

Opening times
Sat.–Thurs. 8–4 p.m.
For non-Moslems normally
admittance only in the
morning.
Closed on Fri. and Moslem
holy days

Admission charge

The Dome of the Rock is the most important religious building on Haram esh-Sharif but, remarkably enough, is not in the middle (this is taken up by the Chain Dome, see p. 87). The Dome of the Rock is the third, after Mecca and Medina, of the holy places of Islam. It is also the best-preserved and most impressive piece of architecture from the early Islamic period. Its gilded dome is the true symbol of Jerusalem.

The Dome of the Rock was founded by the Omayyad Caliph Abd el Malik (685–705). The inscription inside the Dome gives A.D. 691 as the year of its founding, but also names the Abbasid Caliph el Mamun as the founder. By falsifying the inscription El Mamun, who was not Caliph until 813–833, wanted to immortalise himself as the Dome's founder, but forgot to alter the date.

Exterior

From the outside the Dome of the Rock appears to be an octagonal structure that is perfectly symmetrical in almost every detail. The broad base supports the cupola which rests on a drum and is covered with gilded sheets of aluminium. According to legend the original cupola was covered with 10,000 sheets of pure gold. The first cupola collapsed in 1016 and was later reconstructed with lead sheets. Its present gilded aluminium sheets date from the general restoration of the Dome that was completed in 1963 and to which several Arab countries contributed.

The central circle to which all the individual sections of the

Dome of the Rock: third holiest site in Islam ▶

Dome relate is drawn around the "holy rock". The diameter of the regular octagon is 171 ft/52 m. Each of the outer sides is 65 ft/19·8 m long. All the corners are on the circumference. The four portals are orientated towards the cardinal points and are exactly on the corners of one of the two squares inscribed within the circumference. The elevation of the Dome (height 108 ft/33 m) also follows this principle of the mathematical harmony of all parts.

The exterior of the base is covered with marble up to a height of 18 ft/5·5 m. The upper sections of the base and the drum are decorated with 45,000 faience tiles, some of them bearing verses of the Koran, which in 1963 replaced the previous covering of 16th c. Persian faience tiles.

Interior of the Dome of the Rock

The entrance to the interior, its floor covered with valuable carpets, is through the W portal (remove shoes!)

The Dome is based on a central plan and almost all of it is visible as soon as one enters.

Light enters through the large round-arched windows of the base and through the smaller round-arched windows of the drum below the cupola. From the outside one can also recognise the windows of the base by their arches. The drum, on the other hand, has no window-openings on the outside. The light filters in through holes in the pottery tiles. There is also some stained glass that has survived from the 16th c. The effect of the incoming sunlight can be breathtaking, especially in the afternoon.

The holy rock

In the centre the "holy rock" (about 56 ft/17 m long, about

Fascinating mosaics inside the cupola of the Dome of the Rock

Dome of the Rock

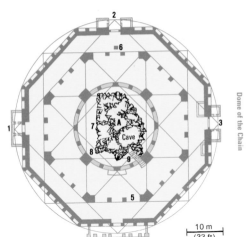

A Holy rock (Es-Sakhra)

1 West Door (Bab el Gharb)
2 Door to Paradise (Bab ed Jenneh)
3 David's Gate of Judgement (Bab es-Silsileh)
4 South Door (Bab el Qibleh)
5 Prayer Niche (Mihrab)
6 Slab which covered Solomon's tomb and into which Mohammed is said to have knocked 12 gold nails
7 Fingerprints of the Archangel Gabriel who is said to have held back the rock when Mohammed ascended into Heaven
8 Footprint of a prophet
9 Steps to the "Fountain of Souls" (Bir el Arwah)

43 ft/13 m wide) projects almost 6·6 ft/2 m above the floor, surrounded by a beautifully carved rail (the Crusaders' iron grille is in the Islamic Museum, see p. 91).

This golden-yellow rock, from which the Dome gets its name, is supposed to be the summit of Mount Moriah, where Abraham was prepared to sacrifice his son Isaac, where the altars of the First and Second temples were supposedly located and where Mohammed took off on his nocturnal ride up to heaven.

According to Moslem tradition, on Mohammed's ascension the rock broke loose in order to follow the prophet. However, the Archangel Gabriel pushed it back into place again and the guides, if asked, will point out the hoof-marks of the prophet's horse and finger-prints of the Archangel. The reliquary shaped like a tower at the edge of the rock contains two hairs from the beard of the prophet.

It is thought that the illuminated hole in the rock was once the means by which water and blood drained off the sacrificial altar and down into the "Fountain of Souls" (see below) which is the source of the light in the hole.

Above the rock is the arch of the cupola (diameter 77·7 ft/23·7 m) decorated with arabesques. The mosaics on a gold ground in the drum mostly depict plants (to prevent idolatry Islam forbids the representation of living beings).

The rock is surrounded by two concentric colonnades of pillars and columns with gilded capitals. The inner circle consists of 12 columns of different designs linked by arches and interspersed with marble-clad pillars. The outer circle is formed by 16 columns linked by architraves and eight angular pillars. Both ambulatories have wooden ceilings.

Fountain of Souls

Stairs lead from the inner ambulatory to the "Fountain of Souls" (Bir el Arwah) situated immediately beneath the rock, its floor covered with straw matting. This grotto bears the name of "Fountain of Souls" because Moslems believe that the dead pray here twice a week.

It is probably a former cistern. The hole in the roof is thought to be the gutter draining from the former sacrificial altar.

Below the "Fountain of Souls" is another grotto known as "the Jaws of Chaos" which has a brick-covered ceiling. This grotto is linked to Jerusalem's network of canals. Many think they can hear the rivers of paradise in the sound of the rushing water.

Domed buildings N of the
Dome of the Rock

There are other domed buildings in front of the N portal of the Dome of the Rock, some of them on the platform.

Prayer niche of the prophet

Just by the N portal is the Prayer Niche of the prophet (Mihrab en-Nebi), a 16th c. building.

Ascension Dome

A little further NW stands a large octagonal domed building, the Ascension Dome (Qubbat el Miraj). It is connected with Mohammed's nocturnal ride up to heaven.

The building dates from the 13th c. During the Crusades it may have been used as the baptismal chapel of the Templum Domini. The preferred shape for Christian baptistries was an octagon.

Hebron Dome

Further NW is the Hebron Dome (Qubbat el Khalili), dedicated to Abraham, which was built in the 19th c.

Dome of St George

In front of the arcade of steps in the NW corner is the Dome of St George (Qubbat el Kadr), also known as the Elijah Dome.

Dome of the Spirits

In front of the arcade there is also the Dome of the Spirits (Qubbat el Arwah), a 15th c. building. This is where the spirits of dead Moslem saints gather at night.

The staircases on the N side of the platform lead to the Dome of Suleiman (Qubbat Suleiman) on the left and the Dome of the Prophet (Qubbat en-Nebi) on the right.

Throne of Solomon

The little mosque on the E wall is built over the so-called "Throne of Solomon". This is where Solomon is said to have followed the building work on the Temple.

Not far from Solomon's Throne is the Golden Gate.

Golden Gate (Sha'ar Ha Rahamim)

The Golden Gate, walled up for centuries, is the best-preserved and the most shrouded in myths of the eight gates of the Old Town. As a symbol of the Virgin it was of fundamental importance for Christian art in the Middle Ages.

Strictly speaking it is not one of the gates of the Old Town, since it is at the back of Haram esh-Sharif, but the E wall of the holy precinct also functions here as a wall of the Old Town.

Steps lead down to the gate. The difference in levels indicates the fact that the sides of the precinct had to be shored up after the gate was built.

The Golden Gate had two archways through it and was three transoms deep. The architecture and the ornamentation of the arches, pilasters, capitals, cornices and achitrave suggest that it dates from the end of the early Byzantine era, but fragments

The Golden Gate: the Old Town gate shrouded in myths

dating from the time of Herod the Great have also been discovered.

Two events that took place at the end of the early Byzantine era are advanced as more or less equally valid reasons for the building of the gate.

Eudocia, wife of Emperor Theodosius II, settled in Jerusalem in 444 and ordered the reconstruction of the E wall of the Temple facing the Mount of Olives. The gate was built to commemorate the healing of the lame by Peter (the Golden Gate was considered to be the successor to Herod's "Beautiful Gate"). A man who had been lame from birth was laid every day at the "Beautiful Gate" of the Temple to beg for alms. Peter did not give him alms but healed him instead (Acts 3).

The second version is linked with the capture of Jerusalem by the Persians, which also occurred at the end of the early Byzantine era (614). Emperor Herakleios I visited Jerusalem in 629 after the Persians had left the city. The Golden Gate is thought to have been built for the entry into the city of the emperor who had recovered the "True Cross" from the Persians.

The first occasion on which the gate was walled up is linked with Emperor Herakleios I's entry into the city. When the emperor was about to ride into Jerusalem through the Golden Gate with the "True Cross", "the stones of the gate suddenly fell down and closed one upon the other as though to wall it up. The angel of the Lord appeared above the gate and everyone was afraid. He took the sign of the Cross in his hands and spoke thus: 'As the King of Heaven passed through this gate to his pain and suffering he rode humbly on an ass and not in royal

Christian tradition

85

majesty. Thus he gave an example of humility to those who pray to him.' With these words the angel vanished. Then the Emperor wept bitterly and took off his shoes, laid aside all his garments, even unto his shirt and took up the Cross of the Lord and carried it in humility to the gate. And lo, the hard stones heard the word of the Lord, and the walls rose up again to their former state and there was an entry open for all men.'' (Legenda Aurea).

Christ's entry into Jerusalem is also linked with this gate. In His time the "Beautiful Gate" was part of Herod's Temple precinct (it led from the Courtyard of the Heathens into the Women's Courtyard). Jesus rode on an ass from the Mount of Olives into the city accompanied by those of low birth joyously waving palms (Palm Sunday), to the annoyance of the priests and the occupying Romans. Two of the Evangelists report how Jesus then went to the Temple (to which the Beautiful Gate leads) to drive out the merchants (Matthew 21, Luke 19; Mark 11 has the purification of the Temple taking place a day later).

Christ's entry into the city and the walling up of the gate were foreseen in the following vision of Ezekiel (6th c. B.C.): "Then he brought me back the way of the gate of the outward sanctuary which looketh toward the east; and it was shut. Then said the Lord unto me; This gate shall be shut, it shall not be opened, and no man shall enter in by it; because the Lord, the God of Israel, hath entered in by it, therefore it shall be shut.'' (Ezekiel 44:1–2).

Jewish tradition

According to Jewish tradition the gate will remain shut until the "end of the days", then this is where the Messiah will enter. On their tour round the city walls Jewish pilgrims therefore stopped at this gate to beseech God for mercy at the Last Judgement. It is on these grounds that it is also called "the Gate of Mercy".

Moslem tradition

In 638 Caliph Omar captured the city and declared the square to be a holy precinct of Islam. It is said that the gate remained closed to all unbelievers, except for the two days in the year when it was opened to Jews and Christians – Palm Sunday and the Raising of the Cross.

In 1530 the gate was finally walled up. Some say, maliciously, that the Moslems walled it up to stop the Jewish Messiah from entering. They also say that the Moslem cemetery outside the gate was put there for the very same reason since no Messiah, because of the Jewish rules of cleanliness, could walk over a cemetery.

Yet the Moslems, too, link this gate with their concept of the end of the world: the Righteous will pass through on one side ("Gate of Mercy") and the other will serve as the "Gate of Atonement".

Porta Aurea

It is not the actual stone gate but what it symbolises that gave rise to countless tales and made it a basic motif of Christian art in the Middle Ages.

The Golden Gate is not only the gate where Peter healed the lame man, through which Jesus rode into the city and through which the Messiah will come on Judgement Day, it is also the "Golden Gate" where the aged Joachim and his childless elderly wife Anne met after the angel had promised the birth of Mary (Apocrypha, Gospel of St James). This gate, richly gilded according to legend, later became a symbol of the Immaculate

Conception. Not only did Mary conceive Jesus "immacu-
lately", but Mary herself was a "gift from God and not the fruit
of physical lust".

Mary was given the name of "porta aurea" and was depicted
symbolically as a golden gate. Mary was the Golden Gate
through which Jesus came, unsullied, into the world.

Countless Gothic churches and cathedrals had portals
signifying the "Golden Gate", i.e. signifying Mary as the
Golden Gate. The figures of Mary on the pillars of the trumeaus
of Gothic cathedrals also often originate from this conception
of Mary as the woman who is the Golden Gate.

Chain Dome

On the E side of the platform in front of the Dome of the Rock
is an open domed building with two circular colonnades (11
columns in the outer circle, six in the inner) which looks like a
miniature version of the Dome of the Rock. This is the Chain
Dome (Qubbat es-Silsileh).

What the spiritual central point of the colonnades is meant to
signify is not clear. Yet it is remarkable that the Chain Dome is
exactly in the centre of Haram esh-Sharif, the place that one
would expect the Dome of the Rock to occupy.

Neither is there any exact information about when it was built
or why. The Chain Dome was probably built (as was the Dome
of the Rock) under Caliph Abd el Malik (685–705) (presumably as a treasury). A 10th c. description mentions 20 columns,
so the Dome must have been substantially altered. The
Crusaders turned it into a chapel which they dedicated to the
Apostle James the Younger, the first bishop of Jerusalem.

The arcades on the S side of the platform are the oldest "scales"
(see p. 79). They date back to the 10th c. Near the middle
arcade is a beautiful marble pulpit (14th c.) with steps leading
up to it.

El Kas

The middle staircase leads down to the round basin of El Kas.
This is where the Moslems carry out their prescribed ablutions
(face, hands, feet) before entering the El Aqsa Mosque.

For reasons of hygiene the water must not be scooped out of
the basin, which is why there is a grille round it. Around the
basin is a circle of low stone seats with a water-tap in front of
each one.

El Aqsa Mosque

On the S side of Haram esh-Sharif, facing Mecca, is
Jerusalem's largest mosque, the El Aqsa. It is 262 ft/80 m long
and 180 ft/55 m wide. The contrast between its silver cupola
and the golden cupola of the Dome of the Rock is a
characteristic feature of the Haram esh-Sharif panorama and
the Jerusalem skyline.

El Aqsa means "furthermost point". This means it was the
furthest point the prophet Mohammed reached when his
miraculous horse Baruk ("Lightning") brought him in one day
from Medina to Mount Moriah, where at night he rode up into
heaven (see above, Dome of the Rock: holy rock).

Opening times
Sat.–Thurs. 8 a.m.–4 p.m.
For non-Moslems normally
admittance only in the
morning.
Closed on Fri. and Moslem
holy days

Admittance charge

El Kas: Basin for ritual ablutions

El Aqsa Mosque: the silver cupola and the main portal

There is hardly anything left of the first mosque to be built on this site. In 670 there was a large wooden building here that held 3000 of the faithful. This mosque, known as the Mosque of Omar (the name often given erroneously to the Dome of the Rock), was built on the ruins of the buildings of Herod the Great and the Romans.

Because of the many serious earthquakes reconstruction work and alterations were carried out under the Caliphs Walid I (705–715), el Mansur (754–775) and el Mahdi (775–785). In 1033, under the Fatimid ez-Zahir, the mosque was rebuilt in its present style with seven naves (under el Mahdi it had 15 naves).

In 1099 the Crusaders conquered Temple Mount and converted the mosque into a church which they called the Templum Domini ("Temple of the Lord"), Templum Salomonis ("Temple of Solomon") or Platatium (since this is where the Crusaders first established their residence). They added other buildings in the W (today the Islamic Museum) and in the E (today the Women's Mosque).

After Sultan Saladin captured Jerusalem in 1187 the building reverted to its original function. All the Crusader buildings were demolished except the above mentioned additions in the E and W.

The entrance to the mosque is formed by a seven-arched porch, the central vault of which is higher and wider than the others. The arches correspond to the seven naves of the mosque.

The building materials date from various periods. Some of the lower sections still date from the time of Herod. As one enters, the latest acquisitions added during the most recent restoration work between 1938 and 1942 are immediately apparent: 12 smooth, cool columns of Carrara marble presented by Mussolini. The columns support a ceiling which was a gift from King Farouk of Egypt (1936–52).

Each of the seven naves is eight transoms long. Over the last transom of the central nave is the mosaic-covered cupola. The section under the cupola is separated from the rest of the nave by a triumphal arch also decorated with mosaics.

Right against the S wall (towards Mecca) is the prayer niche (mihrab) flanked by charming little columns. The mosaic decoration dates from the time of Saladin.

To the right of this is an ebony pulpit inlaid with ivory and mother-of-pearl (1168). In 1969 it was set on fire by a fanatical tourist, a young man who believed he must destroy all "heathen filth" on Temple Mount to bring about the coming of the Messiah. The pulpit (fine carvings) has now been restored.

Next to the pulpit are two prayer recesses. One is dedicated to Moses and the other to Issa (Jesus).

White Mosque

In the W transept are the so-called Columns of God's Judgement. Anyone passing beyond them is supposed to succeed in entering Paradise.

This extension, added by the Crusaders, is also called the "Fencing School of the Templars" and is probably where they prayed. Today it is called the "White Mosque" or "Women's Mosque" (Jami en-Nisa) and, as its name suggests, is accessible only to women.

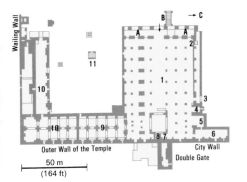

El Aqsa Mosque

A Porch
B Staircase to Basement
C Staircase to "Christ's cradle"

1 Prayer Room
2 Well
3 Elias Gate
4 Prayer Recess of Zachariah
5 Mosque of the 40 Martyrs
6 Omar Mosque
7 Prayer Niche (Mihrab)
8 Pulpit
9 White Mosque (Women's Mosque)
10 **Islamic Museum**
11 Jussef Dome

Christ's Cradle

Near the El Aqsa Mosque in the SE of Haram esh-Sharif steps lead down into a crypt known as "Christ's Cradle". Mary is said to have stopped here after the baby Jesus was presented in the Temple. The "Christ's Cradle" on display is a clam shell dating from Roman times.

From "Christ's Cradle" a broad staircase leads into the underground "Solomon's Stables". The site covers an area of 598 sq. yd/500 sq. m and consists of 13 parallel aisles. 88 pillars in 12 rows support the vaulting. It is known that there are sections dating from the time of Herod the Great, Emperor Justinian and the Crusaders, but no systematic investigations have yet been carried out.

Solomon's Stables

The name "Solomon's Stables" is erroneous. It is thought that at the time of the Second Temple the pens for the sacrificial animals were situated here but the only certain fact is that the Crusaders used them as stabling in the 12th c. The rings for tethering the horses can still be seen on the corners of the pillars.

Islamic Museum

The W transept of the El Aqsa Mosque and an adjacent building house the Islamic Museum.
This contains rich collections of Islamic art, medieval manuscripts of the Koran, other manuscripts, 16th c. glazed tile inscribed with verses from the Koran, etc.
On the far side of the Islamic Museum a ramp leads to the Wailing Wall (see entry).

Opening times
Sun.–Thurs. 10 a.m.–1 p.m., 3.30–6 p.m., Sat. 10 a.m.–1 p.m.

◄ *Interior of the El Aqsa Mosque: cool marble*

Inside the Islamic Museum on Harem esh-Sharif

Hebrew University   F/E3/4

Location
Givat Ram

Telephone
88 28 11

Guided tours
Sun.–Fri. 9–11 a.m. starting
from the administration
building

In addition to the university buildings themselves the large campus of the Hebrew University in Givat Ram also contains the Wise Auditorium, the Williams Planetarium (well worth a visit), the National and University Library, the interesting University Synagogue and students' residences.
When, after the disturbances in 1948, the Hebrew University on Mount Scopus (see entry) became an enclave, accessible only once a fortnight by armoured vehicles that had to cross Arab territory, teaching on Scopus was suspended and the new University Quarter was founded in Givat Ram opposite the Knesset (see entry) and the Government district. Here is also situated the private archive of Albert Einstein (1879–1955).

Hebrew University on Mount Scopus

See Mount Scopus

Hebron (El Khalil)

Buses
From the Damascus Gate,
from the Main Bus Station in
Yafo Road

Hebron is equally holy to Christians, Jews and Moslems as the burial place of Abraham, the patriarch, the "friend of Allah". The Moslem name for Hebron is therefore simply El Khalil, "the friend".

At 3039 ft/926 m above sea level Hebron is one of the highest towns S of Jerusalem. Almost all of its inhabitants are Arab but an Israeli settlement was founded in 1970.

Here Abraham bought the Machpelah cave for the burial of his wife and half-sister Sarah (Genesis 23). Later Abraham himself (25:9–10) was buried here, as were Isaac, Rebecca, Leah and Jacob (49:29 et seq.).

At the time of the conquest of Canaan Hebron was a royal city (Joshua 12:10). David resided here for seven years as king of Judah before he was anointed – also in Hebron – king of the whole of Israel (2 Samuel 5:1 et seq.).

The area (213×115×49 ft/65×35×15 m) above the Machpelah Cave, surrounded by a wall unmistakably in the Herodian style, is reached by means off the NW steps. The N part of the shrine is occupied by a Crusader church which has been converted to a mosque. The church has a nave and two aisles and contains a magnificently carved 12th c. pulpit which is worth seeing.

The various sepulchral monuments and mausoleums, all in different styles, were built above what is supposedly the true tomb in the Machpelah Cave which is not open to visitors. The last person to climb into the cave was the Augustinian monk Arnulf in 1119. He found skeletons which were assumed to be those of the patriarchs and their wives.

Leaving the shrine through the Women's Mosque with the tiled prayer recess the visitor passes the tomb of Joseph the carpenter (Jousef el Majjai), a Moslem saint who is constantly confused with Joseph, the son of Jacob. However, the latter, "the Egyptian", is buried near Sichem (see Nablus).

Location
22 miles/35 km S

Machpelah Cave

Opening times
Sun.–Thurs. 7.30–
11.30 a.m., 1–1.30 p.m.,
4–5 p.m.

---

*Herodion

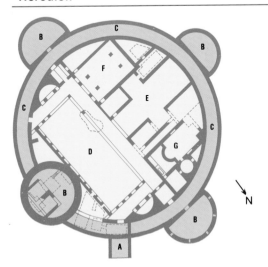

Herodion

The fort was called **Jebel Furadis** by the Arabs. During the Crusades it was called **Frakenberg**, since it was from here that the Crusaders are said to have made their last stand against the Arabs who were harrying them.

A Access Ramp
B Defensive Towers
C Double Wall in form of a circle, with the gangway between the walls used as stores
D Peristyle (stoa)
E Synagogue (erected by the Zealots, later used as a church; cloister garth)
F Synagogue (formerly a Triclinium; dining hall)
G Hot Baths

Herod's Family Tomb

Location
12¼ miles/20 km S

Herod the Great had the luxurious fortress of Herodion built to commemorate his victory over the Hashmonean king Antigonos (37 A.D.). At the same time he had his own mausoleum built here. Josephus Flavius describes how the king's body was carried from Jericho (see entry) to Herodion, but Herod's tomb has yet to be discovered.

To enable the massive building to be constructed Herod had to have the mountain completely reshaped. Situated near Bethlehem (see entry) and shaped like a volcano with its crater levelled off at the top, it is easily recognisable from various vantage points in Jerusalem. The circular double wall with its four round towers contained a three-storey palace and fort with living quarters, baths, porticos, gardens, tombs and buildings for staff and guests.

Herod's Family Tomb   E/F7

Location
Aba Siora

Buses
5, 6, 18

The tomb, near the King David Hotel, was discovered in 1892. According to the description that Josephus Flavius gives in his "Jewish Wars" it could be Herod's family tomb but there is no inscription or other indication that Herod had his sons, grandchildren or other relatives buried here.

The site dates from the 1st c. B.C. The narrow entrance was closed by a round stone which can still be seen. Four sepulchral chambers are hewn out of the rock around a small central room. These chambers (three square, the fourth rectangular) face the cardinal points and are lined with huge square blocks of stone. Two sarcophagi were found here and these are now in the Greek Orthodox patriarchate.

The site belongs to the Greek Orthodox community and they have dedicated a small church here to St George.

Herod's Gate   D8

Location
Sultan Suleiman Road

Opening times
Wall: Sun.–Fri.
10 a.m.–4 p.m.

Herod's Gate, constructed under Suleiman the Magnificent during the building of the wall in 1537–40, is the third entrance from the N to the Old Town after the New Gate and the Damascus Gate (see entries). The official name is Bab ez-Zahrich or Sha'ar Ha-Perahim: "Flower Gate". It is called Herod's Gate because a street is supposed to have run from here to the palace of Herod Antipas.

Hinnom Valley

See Kidron Valley

House of Annas

See Armenian Quarter

In front of Herod's Gate the familiar bazaar atmosphere and colourful crowds ▶

Islamic Museum

See Haram esh-Sharif

*Israel Museum   F4

Location
Newe Sha'Anan/Newe
Grandt, Derekh Ruppin

Buses
9, 16, 24

Opening times
Sun., Mon., Wed., Thurs.
10 a.m.–5 p.m., Tues.
4–10 p.m.
Shrine of the Book 10 a.m.–
10 p.m., Fri. and Sat.
10 a.m.–2 p.m.; Billy Rose
Garden 10 a.m.–sunset

The Israel Museum was opened on 11 May 1965. It is made up of the Samuel Bronfman Museum for Biblical Archaeology, the Bezalel National Museum, the Children's Museum, the Billy Rose Garden and the "Shrine of the Book". The first three of these are housed in the main building which was designed by the architects Alfred Mansfield and Dora Gad. Guided tours in English are given free of charge on Sundays to Thursdays at 11 a.m. and on Tuesdays at 4.30 p.m. Tickets for Saturdays and public holidays must be obtained in advance. To view the collections in the Shrine of the Book you must ask at the desk when buying a ticket of admission.

Samuel Bronfman Museum

The Samuel Bronfman Museum for biblical archaeology contains excavation finds, Jewish ritual objects and Jewish art, decorative items and costumes of the various Jewish communities. An original synagogue from Vittorio Veneto (Italy) and a tabernacle from Horb (West Germany) are on display.

Bezalel National Museum

The displays of paintings in the Bezalel National Museum are frequently changed but those on permanant exhibition include works by Cezanne, Chagall, van Gogh, Gauguin and Picasso among others.

Billy Rose Garden

The garden of sculptures donated by Billy Rose and named after him was chiefly designed by the sculptor and architect Isamu Noguchi. Works by Rodin, Lipchitz, Picasso, Henry Moore, David Smith, Maillol and other famous artists are on display.

Children's Museum

The Children's Museum has an exhibition area, an auditorium and four large workrooms in which young people aged 6–18 can take part in a variety of activities (painting, modelling, graphics, pottery, dancing, archaeology, photography, etc.). There is a playground in the inner courtyard.

The Shrine of the Book

The monument with the most striking and impressive interior and exterior in the grounds of the Israel Museum is the Shrine of the Book. Its white dome is shaped like the lid of one of the jars in which the "Dead Sea Scrolls" were discovered. It was designed by Frederick Kiesler and Armand Bartos. The famous scrolls from the Qumran caves on the Dead Sea (see entry) and other ancient scripts found in caves in the desert are on show in glass cases. In front of the steps leading down to the entrance of the Shrine stands a high wall of black basalt. The contrast with its pale surroundings is intended to symbolise the "Battle of the Sons of Light with the Sons of Darkness".

Library

The library, donated by the German publisher Axel Springer, which houses about 50,000 volumes and a hall with seating for 400, was opened in 1968. In the evenings films are shown and concerts take place.

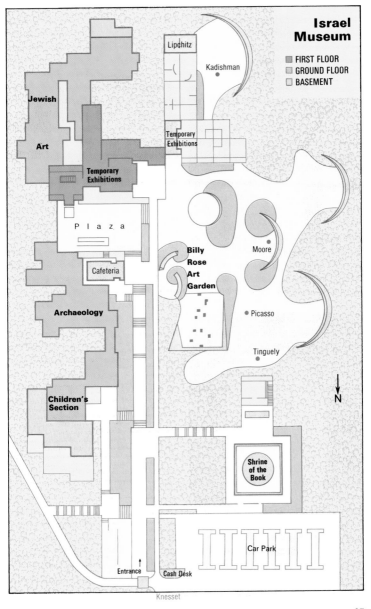

Israel Museum

■ FIRST FLOOR
■ GROUND FLOOR
□ BASEMENT

Lipchitz

Kadishman

Jewish

Art

Temporary
Exhibitions

Temporary
Exhibitions

P l a z a

Cafeteria

Billy
Rose
Art
Garden

Moore

Archaeology

Picasso

Tinguely

N

Children's
Section

Shrine
of the
Book

Car Park

Entrance   Cash Desk

Knesset

Modern Art in the Billy Rose Sculpture Garden in the Israel Museum

Ancient Jewish clay jar in which scrolls were hidden

Shrine of the Book: the most striking building in the Israel Museum

Show case of finds from Qumran in the Shrine of the Book

Jacob's Well

See Nablus

Jaffa Gate   E7

Location
Hativat

Buses
2, 13, 19, 20, 23

Opening times
Wall: Sat.–Thurs. 9 a.m.–
5 p.m., Fri. 9 a.m.–3 p.m.

The Jaffa Gate leading into the Armenian quarter was erected during the building of the wall under Sultan Suleiman the Magnificent. One of its two inscriptions gives 1538 as the date of its construction.

The gate is so named because it was the start of the trade route from Jerusalem to Jaffa, once the most important harbour in the country, and to the Mediterranean coast.

The Arabic name is Bab al-Khalil, "Gate of the Friend", and alludes to the patriach Abraham who is highly honoured by the Muslims. The second inscription then reads: "There is no God except Allah and Abraham is his friend" (cf. the Arabic names of Hebron, see entry).

During the visit of the German kaiser Wilhelm II in 1898 – the year of the opening of the Lutheran Church of the Redeemer – part of the town wall between the Jaffa Gate and the Citadel (see entry) was pulled down so that the illustrious guest could enter the town more comfortably by coach. About 275 yds/250 m south of the Jaffa Gate lies the so-called "Hutzot Hayotzer", a street containing many art and craft shops.

Jason's Tomb   F5

Location
Alfasi Road

Buses
9, 19, 22

Opening times
Mon., Thurs. 10 a.m.–1 p.m.

An inscription on the interior of this pyramidal tomb gives the name of its builder. Next to it are charcoal drawings of boats. Jason had the tomb constructed towards the end of the 2nd c. B.C., that is at the time of the Hashmoneans. Interestingly, there is a reference in Maccabees to the fact that Simon, who was himself a Maccabee – the dynasty was later designated "Hashmonean" – also used the motif of boats in decorating his father's tomb (1 Maccabees 13:29).

*Jericho

Location
22 miles/35 km NE

Buses
From Damascus Gate

Jericho is the oldest known city in the world – a settlement existed here as early as the 10th–8th millennia B.C. It lies 812 ft/250 m below sea level and owes its tropical climate to this sheltered position. In summer the countryside becomes a blossoming oasis in the midst of desert and abundant fruits and flowers flourish here.

There is a very mild climate in winter – Herod had his winter residence built near Jericho.

At the time of the Judges (1200–1000 B.C.) Jericho was called "City of Palm Trees" (5 Moses 34:3; Judges 3:13). The city was later repeatedly destroyed but, because of the fertility of the land, it was always rebuilt again. The Roman triumvir Mark Antony made a present of the bountiful town to his lover Cleopatra, who in turn leased it out to Herod. Herod built his winter residence, the Kypros Castle, a hippodrome, an amphitheatre, magnificent gardens, baths and aqueducts here. He died here and his body was transferred to Herodion (see entry).

The Jaffa Gate: once the start of the Mediterranean trade route

"The Walls of Jericho"

Hisham Palace

Besides Herod's City the following are also worth visiting: Tell
es-Sultan, the mosaics in the synagogue on the Roman street,
which probably date from the 6th c., the "sugar mills" from the
time of the Crusades, and the palace of Caliph Hisham
(mosaics), not far from the Well of Elisha mentioned in the Old
Testament (2 Kings 2:22).

Jericho is surrounded by extensive excavations, but usually
only archaeologists would find a visit to them worth while, and
so only a summary survey will be given here. The literature on
the excavations in and around Jericho would fill entire libraries.

Tell es-Sultan

The most important excavation is that of Tell es-Sultan, a
partially artificial mound on the W side of Jericho. Houses,
remains of walls and a defensive tower 32 ft/10 m in diameter
dating from the 8th millennium B.C. were discovered here. The
Jericho of the Old Testament may also have been sited here.
Jericho's walls collapsed on the seventh day of siege when
seven priests carrying the Ark of the Covenant and blowing
seven trumpets encircled the town seven times (Joshua 6). No
trace of these walls has, however, been discovered.

The Mount of the Temptation

To the W of Jericho lies the "Mount of the Temptation". If you
are prepared for half an hour's walk on a good path you will be
rewarded with magnificent views from the summit.

Greek Orthodox Monastery

The Greek Orthodox Monastery (1874) halfway up the
mountain was erected on the ruins of a Crusader building and
stands on the spot where, according to tradition, Jesus was first
tempted by Satan. A visit to the monastery with its caves, cells,
grottos and paintings is highly recommended.

In the monastery's Church of the Annunciation, consecrated in
1904, 13 steps lead to the "Chapel of the first Temptation".
Jesus was led into solitude by the Holy Spirit but after 40 days
of fasting he was on the brink of starvation. Satan then
approached him and said: "If thou art the Son of God,
command this stone that it become bread." On display in the
chapel is the stone on which Jesus reputedly sat when he
answered Satan: "Man shall not live by bread alone" (Luke
4:4).

Summit

The "Monastery of the Third Temptation" was never completed
but from below the summit of the Mount of the Temptation its
encircling walls make it look like a fortress. (The second
temptation took place on the battlements of the Temple of
Jerusalem.)

It was on the top of this mountain that Satan promised Jesus all
the kingdoms of the world if he would kneel down and worship
him. Jesus, however, replied: "Get thee hence Satan"
(Matthew 4:8 et seq.). Inside the walls stand the ruins of a
Byzantine and a medieval church.

The site of the Syrian stronghold of Dok, in which the
Maccabee Simon and two of his sons were murdered after a
drinking session, has also been located on the top of the Mount
of the Temptation (c. 135 B.C.; 1 Maccabees 16:14 et seq.).
There are magnificent views of Jericho, the Mount of Olives
and the Dead Sea (see entries) from here.

Jewish Agency

E6

The horseshoe-shaped building complex of the Zionist Central Offices house the Jewish Agency, the Keren Kayemet (Jewish National Fund) and the Keren Hayesod (Jewish Foundation Fund). The "Golden Books" in which donors are immortalised are kept in the building which also houses a library and the Zionist archives.

Location
Ha Melekh George

Buses
4, 7, 8, 9, 10, 16, 17, 19

Jewish Quarter

E8

The "Jewish Quarter" in the south of the old town was destroyed during the Israeli–Arab conflict of 1948 and subsequently. Since the reunion of the two halves of the city in 1967 the quarter with its synagogues and Thorah rooms has been rebuilt and made habitable again.

Buses
1, 38

* Kidron Valley

E/F8

The Valley of Kidron of Josaphat, with its tombs, Spring of Gihon and the Pool of Siloah, separates Haram esh-Sharif (see entry) from the Mount of Olives and leads SW past Mount Ophel, the suggested site of the City of David. It then joins the Hinnom Valley – the valley of hell.
Although the name Kidron ("muddy stream") indicates the presence of water, today the valley is dry throughout the year. For a while, at the time of the Evangelists, there seems to have been water here: John speaks of the "brook Kidron" (18:1).

Location
SE of Old Town

Jewish tombs

In the Kidron Valley at the foot of the Mount of Olives, there are numerous graves (see also entry for Mount of Olives: Old Jewish Cemetery and for Tombs of the Prophets) as this was a public burial ground even at the time of the Old Testament kings (2 Kings 23:6). There is a connection between the alternative name, Valley of Josaphat, and these graves. According to the prophet Joel, the Lord will gather together all the nations and bring them into the Valley of Josaphat and will judge them there (3:2 et seq.). It is generally supposed that the Valley of Kidron and the Valley of Josaphat are one and the same. This quotation has been extended and is responsible for the tradition that the Lord will also wake the dead here. Behind the partly ruinous tomb of Josaphat are the four most important burial monuments.

The name "Tomb of Absalom" is misleading. The Hebrew name "Absalom's Monument" accords better with the evidence. Absalom, one of King David's sons, had a memorial erected during his lifetime which "is called Absalom's Monument unto this day" (2 Samuel 18:18). However, the so-called "Tomb of Absalom" actually is a tomb, although it does not date from the time of King David (1004–965 B.C.) but from the 1st c. B.C. This free-standing monument, carved out of the rock right down to its square base, is 65 ft/20 m high and conceals two burial chambers. Absalom rebelled against his father but suffered a crushing defeat and was killed by an officer of his father's

Tomb of Absalom

troops. The soldiers threw his body into a pit in the forest and piled stones on top of it (2 Samuel 18:17). Absalom's tomb and monument are not synonymous.

Bene Hezir Tombs

Not far from the Tomb of Absalom lie the Bene Hezir Tombs. An old Hebrew inscription on the richly decorated architrave tells that this is the family vault of the priestly clan of Hezir. This family is mentioned as having drawn the 17th lot in the rota for temple service at the time of King David (1 Chronicles 24:15). The burial vault dates from the 2nd c. B.C.

The tomb of Zaccariah

This monolithic tomb is carved out of the surrounding rock and has a pyramidal roof supported by ionic columns. Although traditionally associated with the prophet Zaccariah (6th c. B.C.), it dates from the 1st c. B.C.

Gihon

The Spring of Gihon rises in a grotto at the foot of Mount Ophel. It is also known as the "Spring of the Virgin Mary", or as the "Mother of the Steps" (Um el-Daraj), since there are 32 steps leading to it. Gihon means "Springing Up". In former times the water used to shoot up for a few minutes like a fountain and then no water would flow for a few hours. The spring flows in this intermittent fashion all the year round and there is evidence of this as early as the time of Solomon. It was of great importance in providing the City of David with water. Today the flow of water is more regular and less turbulent.

Solomon was anointed king here (1 Kings 1:38) and had a channel dug from the spring into the town. When Sanherib of Assyria conquered the town, King Hezekiah (725–697 B.C.) ordered the spring and channel to be covered over (2 Chronicles 32:30). Perhaps "covering over" refers to the tunnel which Hezekiah had built (2 Kings 20:20). The water from Gihon was brought through a tunnel over 1625 ft/500 m long into the town where it flowed into the Pool of Siloah. The tunnel was driven into the rock by two gangs of workmen and an inscription found in 1880 tells of the meeting between the two groups. It reads: "the rock above the heads of the workmen was 100 cubits thick." Today this, the oldest known Hebrew inscription, is in the Historical Museum of Istanbul.

The tunnel ends in the Pool of Siloah.

Mount Ophel

From the Spring of Gihon steps lead up to Mount Ophel. Here you can visit excavations which are thought to be associated with the City of David.

Mount Ophel borders on to the southern side of the Temple precinct of Haram esh-Sharif (see entry). It is suspected that the early Jebusite town and the later City of David lie within this area. King Jotham (co-regent 756–741 B.C.) built an "Ophel wall" (2 Chronicles 27:3) and King Manasseh (696–642 B.C.) built a ring wall which encircled the Ophel (2 Chronicles 33:14). For over a century people have sought evidence of the tombs of the kings here and also the exact site of the Jebusite city conquered by King David. Tombs have been found, but it is doubtful whether these actually were the burial places of the kings.

Absalom's so-called Tomb in the Kidron Valley ▶

The Pool of Siloah

The tunnel which King Hezekiah had built carried water from the Spring of Gihon into the town and ended in the Pool of Siloah. Today the pool is 52 ft/16 m long, 13 ft/4 m wide and 19 ft/6 m deep but overall considerably smaller than it used to be.

The Christians revere the Pool of Siloah because it was here that Jesus told a man who had been blind from birth to come and wash (John 9:11); whereupon he was given sight. Because of this miracle the water was later considered to have healing properties and numerous sick people came to bathe in it.

In the 5th c. a church was erected here in memory of the healing of the blind man. It was later destroyed by the Persians in A.D. 614. A mosque later stood here, the ruins of which still remain. The ruins of the church, with nave and side aisles, were first excavated in 1896.

The Jews come to the Pool of Siloah to pray on Rosh Hashanah (the start of the New Year, September/October, see Practical Information, Calendar of Events) and in order to celebrate Tashlih at which sins are symbolically thrown into the water, Simhat Bet Ha-Sho'ewa, is also celebrated here. The Pool of Siloah is used to water the so-called "Garden of the King" which is frequently mentioned in the Bible (e.g. Nehemiah 3:15). Today this "garden" is a fertile field.

Silwan

The village of Silwan lies on the northern slopes of the Mount of Offence opposite the Spring of Gihon. Excavations have uncovered a Jewish cemetery here. Christian monks lived in the tombs from the 4th to 7th c. and during the 12th c. Some Christian symbols are still visible. Arabic families settled here in the 16th c. when the village of Silwan grew up.

Foreigners among the 700 chief wives and the 300 lesser wives of King Solomon persuaded the king to worship idols. According to tradition Solomon had shrines built to the Moabite god Chemosh and the Ammonite god Moloch at the request of his foreign wives (1 Kings 11).

Valley of Hinnom

To the S of the Old Town the Valley of Hinnom leads into the Valley of Kidron. The Hebrew name is Ge'Hinnom, from which came the graeco-latin name for hell: Gehenna.

In the Valley of Hinnom stands the infamous Thophet, the altar of burnt offerings where child sacrifices were offered to the Ammonite god Moloch to whom King Solomon had already built shrines (see above, Silwan). These, however, were destroyed by King Hezekiah (725–697 B.C.).

When King Hezekiah's son Manasseh ascended the throne as a 12 year old in 696 B.C. he had the heathen temple rebuilt and constructed places of worship for Baal and for the goddess Astherot who was associated with rites of fertility and love. He sacrificed his own sons to Moloch in the Hinnom Valley and practised divination and magic (2 Chronicles 33).

King Josiah (639–609 B.C.) had these places of worship razed to the ground but the memory of the abomination remained. From then on the word Ge'Hinnom meant "hell" in general, even when not associated with the valley. Even the Moslem name for hell – Ğahannam – is derived from the name of the valley.

Jeremiah prophesied that a time would come when Thophet, altar of burnt offerings, and the Valley of Hinnom would no longer be spoken of, but that they would be called the "Valley of Slaughter". The Jews would then be buried in Thophet because there would be nowhere else to bury them (Jeremiah 7:32).

Hakel Dama

Hakel Dama is the so-called Field of Blood or Potter's Field on the southern slopes of the Valley of Hinnom. After Judas had betrayed Jesus he threw down the 30 silver coins in the Temple and hanged himself. Because this was blood money it could not be put in the Temple treasury, so the priests used the money to buy the field from a potter to make a cemetery there. "Wherefore that field was called, "The field of Blood" (Hakel Dama) unto this day" (Matthew 27:3–8). According to another version Judas bought the field himself with the blood money and then "falling headlong, he burst asunder in the midst and all his bowels gushed out" (Acts 1:18).

Knesset

The Knesset ("Assembly") is the Israeli Parliament. The modern building which was opened in 1966 stands on a small hill in the Hakirya, the government district, opposite the Israel Museum and not far from the Hebrew University (see entry), Givat Ram.

The Menorah, symbol of the State of Israel, stands before the entrance. The seven-branched bronze candlestick depicting events from Jewish history was a present from the British government. It is the work of Benno Elkan.

A flame burns on a small monument in remembrance of those who fell in battle. The heavy iron gate was designed by the Jerusalem artist D. Polombo.

Dominating the entrance hall is a huge image of Theodor Herzl (1860–1904), founder of political Zionism. The triple tapestry in the upper foyer was designed by Marc Chagall and depicts the Creation of the World, the Exodus (flight from Egypt) and the Return. The wall and floor mosaics "The Banishment and the Deliverance" are also the work of Marc Chagall.

The plenary chamber has seating for the 120 members as well as space for reporters. There is also a visitors' gallery. The wall of carved white stone behind the podium was created by Danny Caravan. For the composition of the Knesset elected in 1981 see Introduction, History of Jerusalem.

Passports must be shown when buying tickets for the visitors' gallery, which can be obtained in the Knesset office.

Location
Derekh Ruppin

Bus
9

Opening times
During sittings:
(visitors' gallery) Mon.,
Tues. 4–9 p.m., Wed.
11 a.m.–1 p.m.; tickets from
the office

Free guided tours
Sun. and Thurs. 8.30 a.m.–
2.30 p.m.

Advice

Inside the Knesset, Israel's House of Parliament

The Lion Gate: built after a sultan's dream

Lion Gate (or Stephen's Gate)   D8

The Lion Gate, like most of the gates to the Old Town, was constructed during the building of the Wall from 1537 to 1540 under Sultan Suleiman the Magnificent. An inscription on the arch names the builder.

Of the many names by which this gate is known, the most common are Lion Gate and Stephen's Gate. According to legend the sultan was commanded in a dream to surround the Holy City with a wall and that if he failed to do so, he would be torn to pieces by lions.

The sultan followed the instructions of the dream and added the leonine reliefs from which the gate derives its name. Far more likely, however, is that the lions are devices from the coat of arms of the Mameluke sultan Baybars (1260–77) which Suleiman adopted.

The name Stephen's Gate goes back to a Christian tradition which holds that St Stephen was led through this gate to be stoned to death.

The Moslems named the gate after Mary, mother of Jesus, because the house in which she was born is said to have stood 162 ft/50 m to the W (see Church of St Anne).

Location
E of Old Town

Buses
12, 27

Opening times
Wall: Sat.–Thurs. 9 a.m.–5 p.m., Fri. 9 a.m.–3 p.m.

Massada (Masada, Mezada)

2½ miles/4 km from the Dead Sea (see entry), isolated in the flat plain, stands a mountain 1300 ft/400 m high. Here lie the remains of the fortress of Massada – one of Herod the Great's mightiest and most impressive buildings and scene of one of the most violent tragedies in Jewish history.

Herod built his fortress to be a refuge and a stronghold. He "built a wall of white stone around the top of the mountain which was 7 stadia long (4550 ft/1400 m), 12 cubits high (20 ft/5 m) and 8 cubits thick (13 ft/4 m). On the wall there were 37 towers, each 50 cubits high (81 ft/25 m) through which the buildings within the walls could be reached." These facts, given by the Jewish historian Josephus Flavius, have been more or less borne out by excavation.

Almost all that is known of Massada comes from Josephus Flavius – in many ways more of a storyteller than a historian. However, excavations would seem to support his account of the heroic deaths of the besieged people of Massada in A.D. 73. In order to capture the fortress the Romans set up eight camps at the foot of the mountain. In the face of such a hopeless situation, the besieged people decided they would rather perish together than fall into enemy hands. They drew lots to decide who among the 960 men, women and children should be the first to die and who should put them to death. When almost all of them had voluntarily met their deaths, "they then chose 10 men from among them who were to be the executioners of all the rest. Then each one lay down next to their already dead kin, wife and children, put their arms around them and finally offered up their necks to the men to whose lot this unholy task had fallen. These unwaveringly executed all the others and then drew lots among themselves in the same way. The loser had to kill the other nine and finally deal himself the fatal blow."

Location
25 miles/40 km SE

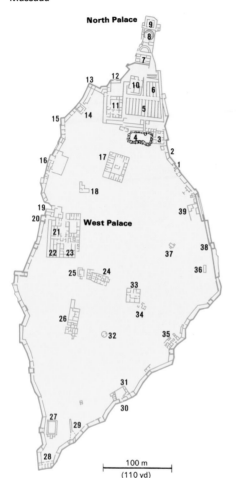

North Palace

West Palace

100 m
(110 yd)

Massada/Masada
Mezada

1 East Gate
  (Snake Path Gate)
2 Casemate Wall
3 Buildings
4 Quarry
5 Storehouse
6 Storehouse
7 Upper Terrace
  of North Palace
8 Middle Terrace
  of North Palace
9 Lower Terrace
  of North Palace
10 Baths
11 Administrative Buildings
12 North Gate (Water Gate)
13 Tower
14 Synagogue
15 Casemate Wall
16 Tower
17 Byzantine Building
18 Church dating from when
   Byzantine monks lived here
   (5th c.)
19 West Gate
20 Tower
21 Administrative Section
   of North Palace
22 Storerooms in West Palace
23 Royal Apartments
   in West Palace
24 Small Palace
25 Ritual Bath
26 Small Palace
27 Cistern
28 South Bastion
29 Underground Cistern
30 South Gate (cistern gate)
31 Ritual Bath
32 Columbarium
33 Small Palace
34 Byzantine Living Quarters
35 Zealots' Living Quarters
36 Cistern
37 Byzantine House
38 Tower
39 Zealots' Living Quarters

Josephus Flavius says that he heard this story from a woman who had hidden herself, together with a companion and five children, in an underground aqueduct. Whether this story be true or not – excavations have uncovered sherds used as lots and each of these bears a different name, although all are written by the same hand.

A detailed description of the fortress of Massada would exceed the scope of this book. A special guide book can be purchased at the gates (available in different languages) in which everything of interest and importance is described at length.

Monastery of the Cross
F5

The massive, windowless walls surrounding the Monastery of
the Cross look like a medieval fortress. They contrast strongly
with the neighbouring modern buildings of the Israel Museum
and the Knesset (see entries).
The monastery was built in the 11th c. by Georgian monks but
stands on the foundations of an earlier Georgian building of the
5th c. It has been frequently restored. When the Georgians fell
into debt they sold it to the Greeks who established a college of
theology (1858).
The floor of the domed church is decorated with mosaics which
date from the early Byzantine period. The wall frescoes depict
the story of the Holy Cross. It is to this story that the monastery
owes its name: according to tradition, the tree grew here from
the timber of which the Cross of Christ was cut. The exact spot
is marked behind the altar.

Location
Sederot Yizhaq Ben Zevi

Buses
9

Opening times
Wed.–Fri. 9 a.m.–1 p.m.,
3–5 p.m., Sat. 9 a.m.–1 p.m.

Monastery of the Olive Tree

See Armenian Quarter

Mosaic of the Birds
D7

In 1894 a 5th c. Armenian mosaic was discovered about 1000
ft/300 m NW of the Damascus Gate (see entry). It could be
considered the oldest memorial to an unknown soldier.
Measuring just 26 ft/8 m × 14 ft/4·30 m, it formed part of a floor
which probably came from a sepulchral chapel for Armenian
soldiers who fell in battle against the Persians in A.D. 451. The
mosaic depicts a huge vine with birds sitting on its branches.
The inscription at the top reads: "To commemorate and bless
those Armenians whose names are known to God alone".

Near here is a sepulchral cave in which human skeletons and
clay lamps of the same period were found.

Location
Between Derekh Shekhem
and Ha Nevi'im

Opening times
7 a.m.–5.30 p.m.

Mosque of Omar
E7/8

To the S of the Church of the Holy Sepulchre (see entry) stands
the Mosque of Omar, a 12th c. building with two minarets (the
minaret in the courtyard is 15th c.). The Mosque of Omar
commemorates the fact that after the conquest of Jerusalem
(638) Caliph Omar prayed here to Jesus. Omar did not enter the
Church of the Holy Sepulchre because he feared that if he did
it might be taken away from the Christians. The tomb in the
Church of the Holy Sepulchre is the only monument connected
with Jesus which the Moslems do not recognise.
On no account should the Mosque of Omar be confused with
the Dome of the Rock (Haram esh-Sharif, see entry) which is
frequently wrongly called the Omar Mosque – even in official
guides and town plans.

Location
Old Town (S of the Church
of the Holy Sepulchre)

Mount Garizim

See Nablus

Mount Herzl   E/F1/2

Location
Sederot Herzl

Buses
12, 18, 20, 21, 26

Opening times
Park:
Summer: 8 a.m.–6.30 p.m.
Winter: 8 a.m.–5 p.m.
Museum:
Sun., Mon., Tues. and Thurs.
9 a.m.–6.30 p.m.; Fri. and
Sat. 9 a.m.–1 p.m.

The tomb of Theodor (Benjamin Seew) Herzl, the founder of
political Zionism, is in a large park on the edge of the suburb of
Bayit We-Gan. There is also a museum here with documents,
books, photographs and Herzl's study (see Introduction,
Famous People).
Every year on the eve of Independence Day (14 May) the
opening ceremony of the national holiday takes place at the
tomb of the Zionist leader. In the W of the park are buried
Vladimir Jabotinsky (1880–1940) and other leaders of the
world Zionist Movement.

Jewish Military Cemetery

Opening times
8 a.m.–sunset daily

The Jewish Military Cemetery is situated on the northern side
of Mount Herzl in a magnificent landscape and is the final
resting place of the Israeli soldiers who gave their lives for the
new state.
From the Jewish Cemetery there is a marvellous view of the
hills of Judea.

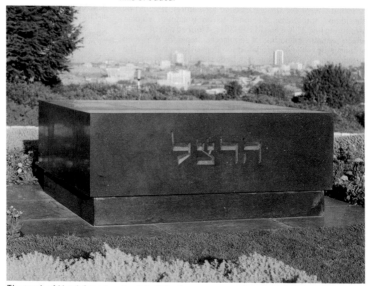

The tomb of Herzl, founder of political Zionism

View over the cemeteries from the Mount of Olives to the Old Town

**Mount of Olives

The Mount of Olives is separated from the town by the Kidron Valley (see entry) through which water once flowed. It forms part of a chain of hills (about 2600 ft/800 m high) to the E of Jerusalem. Because of its height some parts of the mountain afford wonderful views of the Old Town, the Jordan valley and even the Dead Sea (see entry). The mountain's name has remained unchanged for at least 2500 years and derives from the once dense covering of olive trees. Today it is densely covered by a host of shrines, crypts, churches and monasteries, most of which are devoted to the works of Jesus up to his capture. The mountain is mentioned in the Old Testament. After his son, Absalom, had betrayed him, the grieving King David (1004–965 B.C.) climbed up the Mount of Olives and on reaching the summit he prayed (2 Samuel 15:30–2). This passage would indicate that a shrine must have stood here as early as 1000 B.C.

Location
E of Old Town

Bus
42

However, all that is known for certain is that this mountain had always been used as a Jewish burial ground (see p. 118, Tombs of the Prophets). Even today pious Jews still cherish the desire to be buried on the Mount of Olives because, according to tradition, the Messiah will enter Jerusalem from here to awaken the dead. Because of this the Christian and Moslem cemeteries were also sited here. The prophet Zaccariah foretold that: "on that day" the Lord would stand on the Mount of Olives (14:4; see Introduction, Quotations: Zaccariah).

Gethsemane: Which was the tree from which Judas hanged himself?

Before the Temple was destroyed (A.D. 70) fires used to be lit on the Mount of Olives to herald each new moon, i.e., each new month of the Jewish calendar. Later, when the Jews had been forbidden access to the only remnant of their place of worship, the Wailing Wall (see entry), they used to meet on the Mount of Olives. From here the Temple precinct (now Haram esh-Sharif – see entry) could be seen and so it was here that they prayed and that they implored that the Temple be rebuilt.

Gethsemane

Opening times
Summer: 8.30 a.m.–noon,
3–7 p.m.
Winter: 8.30 a.m.–noon,
2–4 or 5 p.m.

At the foot of the Mount of Olives lies the Garden of Gethsemane which is today once again a "real" garden full of flowers. Seven ancient olive trees, which still bear fruit, might still remind the visitor of the reason for the garden's name: "Olive press" (Hebrew: Gat Shehmanim). It is allegedly here that Jesus prayed on the night before he was seized.

Church of the Nations

Opening times
Summer: 8.30 a.m.–noon,
3–7 p.m.
Winter: 8.30 a.m.–noon,
2–4 or 5 p.m.
No admittance if unsuitably
attired

The chief feature of Gethsemane is the "Church of the Nations" which stands within a small fenced garden and is cared for by the Franciscans. Its building was financed by donations from 12 nations. It was also known as the "Basilica of the Agony" and was designed by the Italian architect Antonio Barluzzi in 1924 (he was responsible for almost all the modern churches on the Mount of Olives). This church succeeded the 4th c. "Egeria Church" and the 12th c. Crusader basilica (ruins of both still exist). There is a rock in the nave to mark the spot

where Jesus begged his heavenly father to take the bitter "cup"
of suffering from him (Luke 22:41 et seq.) while his disciples
slept (see page 116, Cave of Gethsemane).

Tomb of the Virgin

The sepulchral church of the Virgin Mary stands on the
opposite side of the road. A church was already standing here,
over the Virgin's tomb, as early as the 5th c. but it fell into the
hands of the Fatimid Caliph al-Hakim in 1009. The Crusader
Godefroy de Bouillon, overseer of the Holy Tomb from 1099 to
1100, found the "Abbey of the Virgin Mary in the Valley of
Josaphat" here and entrusted it to the Benedictines. In 1130
the Crusaders erected the church, parts of which are still
standing today (façade). Following the departure of the
Crusaders this holy site was taken over by the Franciscans who
undertook many of the most urgent repairs.
Since 1797 the Tomb has been in the possession of the Greeks
and Armenians. Lesser rights are enjoyed by Syrians, Copts and
Abyssinians and the Moslems also have an area for prayer. The
Roman Catholics no longer hold services here.

Opening times
Mon.–Sat. 6–11.30 a.m.,
2–5 p.m.

A wide flight of 45 marble steps leads down to the crypt. About
half-way down on the right is the tomb of Melisendis, queen of
Jerusalem from 1143 to 1152 (d. 1161). A little further down
on the left is the vault of the de Bologne family.
The Byzantine crypt is hewn partly from the rock and is in
almost complete darkness. The paintings which adorned the
walls in the 12th c. are no longer apparent.

Crypt

The Church of the Nations on the Mount of Olives

Both the altar on the wall of the tomb and the one opposite it belong to the Armenians. There is a mihrab, a Moslem prayer recess facing Mecca, on the right of the stone tomb. When Mohammed's magic horse Baruk carried him to Mount Moriah in Jerusalem on his way from Medina (the route took him over the Mount of Olives) he noticed a gleaming light over the tomb of his "sister" Mary. Because of this the site is also revered by Moslems.

A few steps lead down to a chapel dedicated to Joachim and Anne, Mary's parents. Opposite is the chapel of Mary's husband Joseph. The huge cistern supported by nearly 150 pillars was discovered during restoration work in 1946.

Cave of Gethsemane

Opening times
Summer: 8.30 a.m.–noon, 3–7 p.m.
Winter: 8.30 a.m.–noon, 2–4 or 5 p.m.

A few steps away from the sepulchral church of the Virgin Mary lies the Grotto of Gethsemane. It is here that the disciples are supposed to have slept while Jesus called upon his Father in despair (see p. 114, Church of the Nations). The cave lies on the route to Bethany, frequently used by Jesus and his disciples (such as when he accepted the invitation of Lazarus, see p. 123, Bethany). It is 56 ft/17 m long, 29 ft/9 m wide and 11 ft/3·50 m high and probably made a very good over-night shelter. The cave has belonged to the Franciscans since 1392 and they have widened and completely altered the entrance. A new floor has been laid and three new altars erected (with frescoes over them).

If the legend is to be believed, then it was near here that Jesus was betrayed by Judas and then taken prisoner.

Church of Mary Magdalene

Opening times
Tues., Thurs. 9–12 a.m., 2–4 p.m.

Halfway up the Mount of Olives and not far from Gethsemane stands the Russian church of Mary Magdalene. Its seven golden cupolas are considered by many to be the most distinctive landmark on the Mount of Olives. Tsar Alexander III founded the church in 1885 in memory of his mother, Maria Alexandrovna. It was built in the Old Russian style of the 16th c. (consecrated 1888).

Although the paintings inside the church are the work of important Russian artists, they do not blend at all well with its style of architecture. The painting behind the altar is by V. V. Vereščagin (1842–1904) and there are several paintings by A. A. Ivanov (1806–58).

Crypt
The Grand Duchess Elizabeth Feodrovna, who was brutally murdered during the Russian Revolution of 1918, is interred in the crypt.

Garden
In the garden of the annexed monastery the remains of an old flight of steps can be seen which used to lead from the town over the Mount of Olives; many Jewish graves have been found there too.

Dominus Flevit: the church with the tear-shaped cupola

Dominus Flevit

The dome of the Franciscan church Dominus Flevit (the Lord wept) is intended to look like a tear. Tradition has it that the church stands on the spot where Jesus stopped on the Mount of Olives before entering Jerusalem and he wept and prophesied the impending destruction of the town (Luke 19:41–4). Dominus Flevit has had a turbulent history. A mosque was built in 1518 to succeed a Crusader building and then the Franciscans constructed their own little chapel here in 1891 following their expulsion.

During the excavations for the foundations of the modern Dominus Flevit Church in 1953, workmen uncovered the remains of a monastic chapel of the 5th c. Today's modern church was designed by Antonio Barluzzi and was built over the earlier chapel, a considerable amount of which remains (floor mosaic in the apse with inscription of the donor, altar). Temple Mount (see Haram esh-Sharif) and the Old Town can be seen through the window over the altar.

Opening times
8–11.30 a.m., 3–5 p.m.

Excavations
The excavations of the sixties uncovered burial chambers, sarcophagi and ossuaries with Hebrew inscriptions. The cemetery, which dates from 135 B.C. to A.D. 300 was later back-filled but important finds are on exhibition in the building next to the cemetery entrance.

The shrines on the Mount of Olives are associated with the events of the New Testament and are supposed to

"Crying Stones"

117

commemorate these. They are not intended as fetishes in themselves, but as places of worship and meditation.

The almost total commercialisation of Holy Sites which has now taken place – and which had already started in the 4th c., present-day methods merely serving to perfect it – is not without its consequences: religious worship and meditation are scarcely possible any longer. Another unpleasant side-effect (caused by the Western brand of mass tourism) is the plague of shabby "dollar hunters" who pester visitors at every turn. They specialise in providing gullible strangers with novel and unexpected titbits of information. The larger their tip, the more rambling and abstruse their explanation.

One may well smile to see at just how many different places (as is often the case in the Garden of Gethsemane) sensationally minded and ingenuous visitors are being shown the tree from which Judas hanged himself. What will certainly come as a surprise is the sight of an entire family next to a wildly gesticulating local, their cameras trained at unlikely stones on the ground. If you ask why, you will become the next victim and, once relieved of your cash, will be told that these are "Crying Stones".

Such "Crying Stones" are no rarity, particularly not in the area of the Dominus Flevit. Before Jesus wept over the fate of the town, he said to the Pharisees, of his disciples, "I tell you that if these shall hold their peace, the stones will cry out" (Luke 19:40). But the disciples did in fact hold their peace and therefore some stones must have cried out. The question is, which ones were they?

You have to part with a fee for every "Crying Stone" that you are shown.

Tombs of the Prophets

Opening times
Sun.–Fri. 9 a.m.–3.30 p.m.

A path leads from the area of Dominus Flevit to the Jewish cemetery and to the Tombs of the Prophets. After descending a flight of steep stone steps the visitor arrives in a vault with two passages arranged in a semicircle in which 36 recesses have been cut. Legend asserts that these are the Tombs of the Prophets (there are other Tombs of the Prophets in the Kidron Valley, see entry). However, this type of shaft grave is only known from the years anno Domini, and the period of the Prophets is the 5th–6th c. B.C.

Entry is free. There is no lighting, so one should go equipped with a torch. However, the attendant there is quite prepared to light the way around for interested visitors and give detailed explanations.

Old Jewish Cemetery

The Old Jewish Cemetery extends beneath the Tombs of the Prophets. Until 1948 the Mount of Olives was the Jewish burial ground and many Jews came to Jerusalem to die and be buried on the Holy Mountain. There is no other place which, on the one hand, is located outside the town and thus complying with the laws of cleanliness for use as a burial place, and on the other so close to the Golden Gate (see Haram esh-Sharif) through which the Messiah will traditionally pass on the Last Day.

In 1948 this section was seized by the Arabs who desecrated the cemetery and took the grave-stones for use as building materials. This cemetery also contains the graves of Jews murdered in 1929 and of those who fell in the battle for the Old Town in 1948.

Mount of Olives: Old Jewish Cemetery

Small stones honouring the dead

Pater Noster Church

When Emperor Constantine built the Church of the Nativity in
Bethlehem and the Church of the Holy Sepulchre in Jerusalem
(from 326), he also wished to build a majestic basilica on the
Mount of Olives, yet another site of a cave shrine. It is in the
grotto beneath the present church that Jesus is supposed to
have prophesied the end of the world and the final judgement
to his disciples (Matthew 24–5, Mark 13). The Eleona basilica
(Olive Basilica), erected in the 4th c., was destroyed by the
Persians in 614, rebuilt by Modestos and then fell again to al-
Hakim in 1009.

Opening times
8.30 a.m.–noon, 3–4.30 p.m.

The Crusaders built a new church which they called "Pater
Noster" because they believed it to be here that Jesus had
taught the Lord's Prayer (Luke 11:2–4 no reference to the
Mount of Olives; Matthew 6:9–13 in the Sermon on the
Mount). This change in meaning obviously came about
because what Jesus was asked "in private" that is, "when they
were alone" (Mark 13:3) was generally not easily understood,
unlike the Lord's Prayer.

By the year 1600 just one column of the Crusader's church still
stood. Today's church was financed by the devout Princess de
la Tour d'Auvergne who visited Jerusalem in 1856. She
allowed herself to be persuaded into buying the plot by F.
Ratisbonne, a former Jew. (The negotiations with the Moslem
owners of the land lasted 12 years.) For eight years after that
she lived in her own wooden house which she had had
specially brought over from France.

In the meantime the French architect Guillermet drew plans for
the new church which was entrusted to the Carmelite nuns in

The Pater Noster Church: built by a pious princess . . .

. . . with the Lord's Prayer in 60 different languages

1874. The princess had the Lord's Prayer inscribed in 60 different languages on plaques in the entrance and in the cloisters.

Crypt
Eighteen steps lead down from the S side of the open courtyard into the Credo crypt. Twelve pillars of semicircular section support the vaulting.

Ascension Chapel

This tiny mosque surrounded by an octagonal courtyard stands on the highest point of the Mount of Olives and commemorates the Ascension of Christ. Inside it a rock bearing the so-called "footprint" of Christ is on display. The Moslem tradition is also that Christ ascended to heaven (to see Mohammed). According to the New Testament Christ ascended into heaven 40 days after arising from the dead. Luke 24:50–1 names Bethany (see p. 123), further E, as the place of his ascension: Acts names a "place on the Mount of Olives" which lay one Sabbath Day's journey ($=\frac{1}{2}$ mile/1 km) away from Jerusalem. This "place" has now traditionally become known as the summit of the Mount of Olives. According to the Russian version, Christ ascended from the spot where the tower of the Russian monastery now stands (see p. 122).
As early as 387 a chapel stood on the site of the present-day mosque. In the 12th c. the Crusaders constructed an octagonal building with pillars at each each corner supporting an open dome. In 1187 this building was converted to a mosque and in 1200 was provided with a new dome which was closed over.

Chapel of the Ascension on the Mount of Olives

Feast of the Ascension
Christians are allowed to celebrate the Feast of the Ascension here every year (40 days after Easter). Iron hooks in the walls of the courtyard serve the dual purpose of holding the canvas awnings and also marking out the exact area allotted to each of the different Christian communities. Altars are set up in the courtyard and Mass is celebrated from midnight through to midday. Some Christian communities are also allowed to hold Mass on other days.

The Alami family who live next to the Chapel of the Ascension act as caretakers for this holy site. In the Alami's house is a small mosque which affords magnificent panoramic views as far as the Dead Sea (see entry).

Russian Monastery

The monastery, church, bell-tower and hostel were built in 1880 and given to White Russian nuns in 1907. The pictures inside the church are largely the work of the nuns themselves. There is a hole in the mosaic floor in which the head of John the Baptist is said to have been found. He was beheaded after Herod Antipas had made a rash promise to Salome in order to persuade her to dance for him and she had demanded the head of John the Baptist (Mark 6:17–29). Since the church stands on the remains of an earlier, 4th c. one, the possibility cannot be discounted that there was already a memorial to John the Baptist here in the reign of Emperor Constantine.
Besides the mosaic, other items of interest include a small museum, a collection of paintings, pictures of the Russian tsarist family and clothes made by the nuns. According to Russian tradition the 195 ft/60 m high, six-storey bell-tower stands on the spot where Christ ascended into heaven. 214 steps lead to the top of the tower. No other point on the Mount of Olives can offer such extensive views. The nuns had to bring the huge bell here themselves from Jaffa harbour because the Moslem workmen refused to transport it.
The nuns sing daily Vespers at 4.30 p.m.

Bethphage

Bethphage, literally "House of the Unripe Figs", is now the name of a building complex belonging to Franciscan monks and consisting of courtyard, small church, cisterns and cemeteries. A church originally stood here to commemorate the meeting of Lazarus' sisters Martha and Mary with Jesus (John 11:20 et seq.). In 1883 the Franciscans built the present-day church on the ruins of this building. According to Christian tradition this is the site of the village of Bethphage to which Jesus sent two of his disciples on an errand to bring him a donkey which no man had ridden and which was tied up at the entrance to the village (Luke 19:29; Mark 11:1 et seq.). Jesus entered Jerusalem riding on the back of this donkey. Since the time of the Crusaders a large stone block has been kept in the church which Jesus supposedly used as a mounting block. The paintings were restored in 1950 and show Martha and Mary's meeting with Jesus (before the raising of Lazarus); the fetching of the donkey and the entry into Jerusalem.

Palm Sunday Procession

Every Palm Sunday (Sunday before Easter) Bethphage sees the start of a great procession in remembrance of Jesus' entry into Jerusalem. This wends its way down the W slope of the Mount of Olives into the Kidron Valley (see entry), then takes the steep path to the Lion Gate (see entry) and finishes at St Anne's Church (see entry). The procession is a great event in which all the Christian communities take part; monks and nuns, young and old, all singing and carrying palm leaves, are joined by bands of musicians.

The route of the procession has been changed time and again over the centuries, mirroring the uncertainty of the tradition and the political situation. In the 4th c. the procession started on the Mount of Olives; in the 8th c. it started from Bethany and finished at the Church of the Holy Sepulchre (see entry). After having been banned under the Fatimid Caliph al-Hakim, with the Crusaders the procession of the Patriarch once again started out from Bethany; the pilgrims waited on the E side of Temple Mount and then proceeded together through the Golden Gate (see Haram esh-Sharif), which was specially opened for the occasion. In 1840 the procession began in Bethany and ended in the Kidron Valley.

Bethany

The name of the present-day village containing the tomb of Lazarus is el-Azarie (El Azariya), a bowdlerised version of Lazareion, the name of a 4th c. Christian settlement known to have stood here. The village in which Lazarus lived was called Bethany.

Jesus and his disciples often went to Bethany to take up the invitations extended by Lazarus and his sisters Martha and Mary (Lazarus of Bethany is not to be confused with the "poor Lazarus"). In Bethany Jesus raised Lazarus from the dead after he had already lain four days in the grave (John 11). The house of Simon the leper was also in this village (Matthew 26:6).

The church historian Eusebius (c. 265–340), bishop of Cassarea from 313, mentions Lazarus' tomb. St Jerome, father of the Latin Church, wrote in 390 that a church had been erected over the grave of Lazarus. The Crusaders built a church over the house of the sisters Martha and Mary and a monastery over the house of Simon the leper.

In the 16th c. a mosque was constructed on the ruins of these buildings and Christians were forbidden access to the tomb of Lazarus. Finally, the custodian of the Holy Land was given permission in 1613 to dig a second entrance to the tomb.

The tomb of Lazarus is in Moslem hands today but is generally open to visitors (entrance from the street down 24 steps).

The modern Franciscan church was built between 1952 and 1954 to plans by Antonio Barluzzi.

Beth Anania

A little further up the mountain lies the excavated area. There is evidence of Jews having lived in this area since the 6th c. B.C. The settlement was abandoned in the Middle Ages.

It was also in the 6th c. B.C. that the Jews returned from Exile in Babylon. The priest and prophet Nehemiah was cupbearer to the Persian king Artaxerxes during the Exile and was sent by him in about 445 B.C. to be governor of Jerusalem. A census in the book of Nehemiah lists a village called Anania (Nehemiah

11:32) which was allocated to the tribe of Benjamin after their return from Exile. "Bethany" may have been derived from the name Beth Anania ("House of Anania").

Mount Ophel

See Kidron Valley

Mount Scopus   B/C9

Location
Mount Scopus

Buses
9, 28

NE of the Old Town on Mount Scopus are the British War Cemetery for those who fell in the First World War, the Hadassah Hospital, the Hebrew University, the Jewish National Library, the Harry Truman Institute and the German Augusta Viktoria Hospital.

Almost all of Jerusalem can be seen from Mount Scopus. Its name is derived from the Greek "Skopein"=to observe, examine, detect. It was from here that the Roman legions stormed Jerusalem and the Crusaders conquered the town.

Hebrew University

The Hebrew University was founded in 1925. It is situated N of the Mount of Olives on one of the higher parts of Mount Scopus. There are magnificent views from here of the Old Town, the Yehuda desert, the Dead Sea (see entry) and the Moab mountains.

In the S of the university grounds is an amphitheatre in which plays and concerts are held in summer. The graves of the Zionist leaders Leon Pinsker (1821–91) and Ussischkin are to be found in the Botanical Garden, as is a cave called after one Nikanor who is said to have built the great gates of the Herodian Temple.

Free tours in English take place from Sunday to Friday at 11 a.m., starting from the Schermann buildings, Allen Bronsman Family Reception Centre.

Hadassah Hospital

The Hadassah Hospital, opened in 1925, is attached to the Hebrew University. The hospital was unusable after the wars of 1948 so the Hadassah Medical Centre (see entry) was built to take its place. After the Six Day War of 1967, however, the building was restored and since then it has once again served its original purpose.

Free tours (which include the Statue "the Tree of Life" by Jacques Lipchitz) in English take place from Sunday to Friday at 9, 10, 11 a.m. and noon.

Mount of Temptation

See Jericho

**Mount Zion   F7/8

Location
Hativat 'Ezyyoni

Buses
1 (to the Wailing Wall), 13,
20, 23 (to Jaffa Gate)

Mount Zion, in the SW of the Old Town, is a popular centre of pilgrimage, especially at Easter, Whitsun and the Feast of the Tabernacle. The site of the Last Supper (Coenaculum); the room in which Jesus washed the feet of his disciples; the Dormitio Church, where the Virgin Mary "fell asleep forever" and the Tomb of David are all situated here. The "Chamber of Martyrs" commemorates the dead victims of the Hitler regime. Mount Zion means "Fortress Mount" and is the name given to all three of the following: the Jebusite acropolis conquered by King David (1004–965 B.C.) and renamed David's City (1 Chronicles 11:4 et seq.); then the "Holy Mountain" (Temple Mount) because the God of Israel had said that he lived on Mount Zion (Isaiah 8:18); and finally the city of Jerusalem (also "heavenly Jerusalem"). Where Mount Zion really stood is open to question. It used to be thought to stand on the site of Herod's palace, hence the name "David's Tower" (see Citadel with David's Tower).

Opening times
Daily till sunset

Dormitio Church

The present-day Dormitio Church (church of Mary's sleep) was built by German Catholics between 1900 and 1910 and was successor to many earlier buildings. According to tradition it stands on the place where Mary, Mother of God, died.
In about A.D. 355 the Byzantines built the "Church of the Apostles" here within a late-Roman building. In 390 it merged with the Hagia Zion, another enormous Byzantine building with 64 columns which was considered as "the Mother of the Churches of Zion" (destroyed in 966). Christ's crown of thorns and whipping post were displayed here. Another attraction for pilgrims were stones with which St Stephen was said to have been stoned. In the year 1100 the Crusaders erected the church Santa Maria in Monte Zion, here. The tradition had been established as early as the 7th c. that the Apostles had founded

Opening times
Daily, closed 12.30–2 p.m.

The Dormitio Church on Mount Zion

the sepulchral church of Mary here. It is also here that the Apostle Matthias is said to have been chosen as Judas' successor and Jesus was said to have appeared to his apostles after his resurrection.

The Crusader church was destroyed by the sultan of Damascus in 1219. All that was left were the Roman synagogue and a chapel, the present-day Tomb of David and the Coenaculum. Because of the amicable relations between Kaiser Wilhelm II and the Turkish authorities, German Catholics were able to lay the foundation stone for the present church on 7 October 1900. The design, in the Romanesque style of the 19th c. is the work of the Cologne architect Heinrich Renard. In 1957 the church was given the rank of Minor Basilica.

Inside the church

The interior of the church is almost completely dominated by magnificent mosaics.

The mosaic of the Madonna with Child on a gold background is the work of the brother Radbod Commandeur O.S.B. (1939). The Greek sentence in the open book reads: "I am the light of the world." The latin inscription reads: "Behold, a virgin will conceive and bear a son and his name will be Emmanuel" (Emmanuel="God with us").

The centre of the mosaic floor is occupied by the symbol of the Holy Trinity: three interlocking circles and the words: "Holy, holy, holy".

The names of the 4 great and the 12 lesser prophets of the Old testament, the 12 apostles, the symbols of the four evangelists, signs of the zodiac and the names of the 12 months of the year surround the sign of the Trinity in concentric circles.

Mount Zion: Dormitio Monastery and interior of Dormitio Church

The mosaic floor was created by Bernhard Gauer after a design by P. Mauritius Gisler of the Dormitio Abbey.

Figures of the prophets Micah, Isaiah, Jeremiah and Ezekiel, Daniel, Haggai, Zaccariah and Malachi stand between the windows.

The central, basal block of the altar is of Westphalian marble with a mosaic of a lamb – symbol of Christ. The back of the altar is decorated with anchors and fishes. The anchor represents hope. The fishes refer to the book of Matthew 4:19 where Jesus is calling his disciples and says: "I will make you fishers of men." During the persecution of the Christians the fish became the sign of Christ. (Fish=Greek ICHTHYS: ICH=Iesous Christos, THYS=Theou Hyos Soter: God's Son, Redeemer.)

Chapels

The upper church contains six chapels: the chapels of St Boniface, St John the Baptist, St Joseph, the Three Wise Men, St Willibald and St Benedict.

Fourteen ivory-coloured reliefs portray miracles and events from the lives of the saints.

Crypt of Mary's Slumber

The religious centre of the basilica the dark crypt of Mary's slumber, decorated with 12 columns. Under the dome is a poignant statue of the sleeping Mary. The mosaic in the dome portrays Christ welcoming his mother's soul.

Six medallions depict famous women from the Old Testament: Eve, Miriam, Jael, Judith, Ruth and Esther.

Each of the six chapels in the crypt is dedicated to two apostles.

The Tomb of David

SE of the Dormitio Church, in the basement of a building crowned by a minaret, lies the Tomb of David. This is really a cenotaph since the actual tomb has not been found. According to 1 Kings 2:10 King David was laid to rest in David's City, that is, "Mount Zion".

The stone coffin stands in front of a semicircular Roman apse which points towards Temple Mount (see Haram esh-Sharif). Crowns and ritual objects ornament the lid.

The Room of the Washing of the Feet

Next to the room containing the Tomb of David is the Room where Jesus washed his disciples' feet. He did this after the Last Super as a sign of humility and service (John 13:4). Today this room houses a synagogue.

Coenaculum

In the same building as the Room of the Washing of the Feet and the Tomb of David, but in an upper storey which is only accessible from the outside, is the Coenaculum, the Room of the Last Supper. According to Mark 14:15 the Last Supper was held in a "large upper room".

After the Ascension of Christ, his disciples returned (one Sabbath Day's journey=$\frac{1}{2}$ mile/1 km) from the Mount of Olives

The empty grave of King David on Mount Zion

The Coenaculum on Mount Zion: scene of the Last Supper

to Jerusalem and made their way to an "upper chamber" where Matthias was chosen (Acts 1:12 et seq.) as Judas' successor. On Whit Sunday "at the same place" tongues of flame appeared and filled the apostles with the Holy Spirit (Acts 2:1 et seq.).

Coenaculum is therefore traditionally seen not only as the site of the Last Supper but also as the room in which Judas' successor was chosen and in which the Holy Spirit appeared as tongues of flame and settled on the apostles' heads.

The room is divided into two aisles and three transoms by cross-ribbed vaulting in Gothic style but individual parts date from different periods.

Chamber of Martyrs

Not far from the Coenaculum is the Chamber of Martyrs, a memorial to the Jewish victims of the Nazi regime.

Women are not admitted into the chamber, the vaults of which are sooty black from the smoke of countless candles. Men are required to wear a head covering. Cremation furnaces used for Jews are set into the walls.

Museum of Armenian Art and History

See Armenian Quarter

Nablus

Nablus is the town which succeeded "Shechem" of the Old Testament and is the capital of the Samarian district. On 2 June 1980 its mayor, Bassam Sheker, one of the most influential Palestinian politicians in Israeli-occupied territory, lost both his legs in an attempted assassination. The culprits have not been identified but Israeli extremists are suspected. Since that date Nablus has been seething with unrest.

Location
Samarian district
37 miles/60 km N

The town was established by Titus in A.D. 72 as a veteran colony and was named Flavia Neapolis in honour of the Flavian emperor Vespasian (A.D. 69–79). The following centuries witnessed violent clashes between Christians and Samaritans. Today there are barely 500 Samaritans.

Shechem

It has been the fate of Shechem to be continually destroyed and tirelessly rebuilt. It was here that the "de facto" division of the Israelite kingdoms took place. After Solomon's death the Shechemites stoned King Rehoboam but he was just able to reach his chariot and escape to Jerusalem (1 Kings 12:18). From then on, however, the kingdom was divided. Jeroboam (926–907 B.C.) was made king of the Northern kingdom and he fortified Shechem and made it his seat.

Not far from the road S of Nablus there are extensive areas of excavation with finds which date, in part, from pre-Israelite times.

Jacob's Well

It was on the E side of Shechem that Jacob set up camp. He proceeded to buy some land and put up an altar (Genesis 33:18–20). According to Samaritan tradition Jacob dug the 97 ft/30 m well single-handed. It was fed by a spring and today an unfinished church stands over it. It was said that it was here that Jesus encountered the Samaritan woman drawing water (John 4:5 et seq.).

Joseph's Tomb

About 2600 ft/800 m N of Jacob's Well a white dome spans the "Tomb of Joseph". It is reputedly here that the son of Jacob found his final resting-place – that son whose brothers had sold him to an Egyptian slave caravan, upon whom great honours had been bestowed abroad and who died at the age of 110. Joseph's bones were carried back from Egypt and were buried in the plot of land which Jacob had bought (Joshua 24:32).

To the right of Jacob's Well stands Mount Ebal, the "Mountain of Curses", to the left Mount Garizim, the "Mountain of Blessings".

Mount Garizim

When they returned from Exile in Babylon the Jews thought of the Samaritans as the "foolish rabble who live in Shechem" (Ecclesiasticus 50:26).

The Samaritans evolved from an intermingling of the Israelites who had not been deported after the fall of the Northern Kingdom and new settlers from Assyria. Because the Samaritans were forbidden to take part in the building of the second Temple in Jerusalem, they erected their own temple on Mount Garizim. It was destroyed by John Hyrkanos in 128 B.C. Emperor Hadrian (post A.D. 135) built a temple to Jupiter on the summit and the Christians later built their church "Of Our Lady" in its ruins. The Samaritans believe that the Shehinah (Holy Ghost) lives on this mountain and they still celebrate their most important ceremonies on its peak. The best known is the Feast of the Passover.

New Gate   E7

Location
Ha-Zanhanim

Buses
2, 13, 19, 20, 23

The New Gate in the wall was not made until 1888. It was built to create an access between the Christian quarter of the Old Town and the new settlement outside the walls. Permission for the building of the gate was granted by Sultan Abdulhamid II and the gate was originally called Bab es-Sultan in his honour.

Pater Noster Church

See Mount of Olives

Pool of Siloah

See Kidron Valley

Qumran

See Dead Sea

*Rockefeller Museum (Archaeological Museum)

The Rockefeller Museum opposite Herod's Gate is one of the most important museums in Israel. It houses finds arranged chronologically from the Stone Age up to the 18th c. and possesses a very comprehensive library.

The Museum was planned, built and fitted out under the British Mandate (1927–9). The large scale of the building and the generous furnishings were made possible by an enormous contribution from John D. Rockefeller jr., from whom the museum took its name.

To list even a tiny fraction of the exhibits would exceed the limits of this guide. The layout facilities finding one's way around. The following are among the most significant of the objects: Roman sarcophagi and sculptures, skulls and Bronze Age weapons, Omayyaden wood carvings, the grave stele of the Egyptian pharaoh Seti I, Romanesque sculptures from the Church of the Holy Sepulchre, Greek and Byzantine pottery, etc. In any case it is worth buying a museum catalogue.

Location
Northern Town
(near Herod's Gate)

Buses
27, 43, 44, 45

Opening times
Sun.–Thurs. 10 a.m.–5 p.m.,
Fri.–Sat. 10 a.m.–2 p.m.

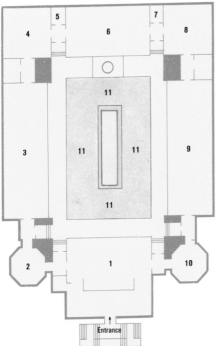

Rockefeller Museum
(Archaeological Museum)

1 TOWER ROOM: Casts of reliefs from the palace of Nineveh which show the capture of Lachish by the Assyrian king Sanherib (701 B.C.).
2 SOUTH OCTAGON: Finds from Egypt and Mesopotamia, among them a stele of the pharaoh Seti I (1319–1304 B.C.).
3 SOUTH GALLERY: Finds from the period 100000 to 1200 B.C., including the Gallilee skull and a copper sword.
4 SOUTH ROOM: 18th c. wood carvings from the El Aqsa Mosque.
5 COIN CABINET: Including Jewish coins of the 1st and 2nd c. A.D.
6 WEST GALLERY: Sculptures from the palace of Qirbat al-Mafyar in Jericho.
7 JEWEL ROOM: Collections from the 18th to the 8th c. B.C., including gold earrings.
8 NORTH ROOM: Sculptures from the time of the Crusades.
9 NORTH GALLERY: Finds from 1200 B.C. to A.D. 1300, also the Lachish letters (pottery sherds with Hebrew inscriptions).
10 NORTH OCTAGON: Jewish objects including menorahs and a mosaic from the synagogue of En Gedi.
11 INNER COURTYARD: Sarcophagi, capitals, mosaics, etc.

Rockefeller Museum: one of Israel's Major museums . . .

. . . with exhibits from the Stone Age to the 18th c.

Russian Compound (Migrash ha Russim)   D7

The large Russian compound on the Yafo Road in the centre of town was bought in 1860 to provide accommodation for Russian pilgrims. The hospice, still standing today, was built in the same year. In the middle of the square stands the Russian Orthodox Cathedral with its green cupola. Near the entrance lies a pillar a good 40 ft/12 m long and fenced around. It is assumed that this was intended for the building of the Herodian temple but broke during transport. Other buildings of the Russian compound house officials, the main post office, police headquarters, etc. The Hall of Heroes commemorates Jewish resistance during the period of the British mandate.

Location
Migrash ha Russim on the Yafo Road

Buses
2, 3, 4, 5, 6, 16, 18, 19, 20

*St Anne's Church   D8

About 150 ft/50 m W of the Lion Gate is St Anne's Church. This Romanesque church stands within a walled area which also encloses a small museum a Greek Catholic seminary and the excavations of the Pool of Bethesda.
Traditionally St Anne's Church stands on the spot where the house of Anne, mother of the virgin Mary, once stood. A St Mary basilica was already built here by the 5th c. – possibly at the command of Empress Eudocia. It was constructed on the ruins of an even older shrine, for it was here that the Virgin Mary was supposed to have been born. After the Persians destroyed the basilica in 614 it was rebuilt by Modestos. The church was completely destroyed in 1009 by the Fatimid Caliph al-Hakim. Other Christian sites in Jerusalem suffered a similar fate at his hands.
The Crusaders built a small chapel over the basilica ruins and in 1140 the present St Anne's Church was erected. It is considered the most beautiful and most characteristic church of the Crusader period, not only in Jerusalem, but in all the Holy Land.
In 1192 Sultan Saladin turned the church into a Moslem school. In 1856 the Ottomans gave the plot to the Catholic "White Fathers" in gratitude for the support of the French in the Crimean War.
The basilica, with nave and side aisles (length 110 ft/34 m, total width just under 65 ft/20 m) and with a dome over pendentives, displays both French and Moslem elements on the exterior and parts of it could be said to resemble a fortress. An inscription over the main portal reminds the visitor that a Koran school was set up here under Saladin. The interior of the church is modestly equipped although there are beautiful frescoes on the walls. It is evident that the building is not quite symmetrical from the position of the window above the altar.

Crypt
Steps lead down to the crypt which is supposedly constructed on the site of the house of Mary and her parents Joachim and Anne. There are the remains of columns, bases, capitals and mosaics dating from Byzantine times.

Location
Old Town, near Lion Gate

Buses
43, 45 (Lion Gate)
12, 27 (Damascus Gate)

St Jacob

Pool of Bethesda

Near to St Anne's Church a double pool has been uncovered which dates from the 1st c.: it is known as the Pool of Bethesda. Excavations carried out since 1871 have shown that the whole installation consisted of five "porches" or colonnades; the pools were separated in the middle by such a porch.

John the Evangelist also speaks of a pool with five porches. In these porches lay the sick, the lame, the blind, etc., each of them hoping to be the first to enter the water when it became troubled, because according to legend an angel came every now and then and stirred up the water. Whoever reached the water first would be healed (John 5:2–4).

It was concluded on the basis of this that these were medicinal healing baths (cult of Asclepius). The name Bethesda, i.e. "House of Mercy" or "House of Compassion", would also point to this. Jesus healed a sick man here who had spent 38 years trying to be first into the water when it became troubled. When Jesus asked him if he wanted to be healed the man answered in the affirmative. Jesus then said to him: "Stand up, take your bed and walk." The Jews, however, took exception to Jesus healing on the Sabbath Day and they also criticised the man who had been healed for carrying his bed (John 5:5–16) on that day.

St Jacob

See Armenian Quarter

Excavations around St Anne's Church

St John in the Wilderness (Monastery)

See En Karem

St John the Baptist

See En Karem and Church of the Redeemer

St Mark (Church and monastery)   E8

The 12th c. church of St Mark, restored in 1940, together with the monastery of the same name, are at the centre of Jerusalem's Syrian Orthodox community.

There are few places in Jerusalem where so many momentous events are said to have taken place in such a small area. Here, it is said, stood Peter's prison; here Peter set up the first church, the Virgin Mary was baptised, the Last Supper took place and here also stood the house of Mary, mother of John the Evangelist, known as Mark.

Peter was taken prisoner under Herod Agrippa I. An angel guided him out of prison and did not leave his side until they had passed the "Iron Gate" into the town. Peter went to the house of Mary, mother of John Mark, where the Christian community gathered (Acts 12:3 et seq.).

Tradition places both the prison and the house of Mary in the same spot. In the 7th c. there was a church here called "Peter in Chains".

The extensive destruction of the church under the 'Abbasid Caliph Harun ar-Raschid (786–809) was followed by the erection of a mosque and a Moslem hospice. Even today, after the restoration of a 12th c. Crusader building, the land next to the monastery is owned by Moslems.

The paintings of the Virgin Mary on the S wall of the church possibly date from the early Byzantine period, but are attributed to Luke the Evangelist.

A small chapel of baptism serves as a reminder that the Virgin Mary was supposedly baptised here. there is a controversy over whether it was Jesus, Peter or John who baptised her. Each candidate has arguments to support him.

Location
SW of Old Town
(St Mark's Road)

Buses
1, 13, 19, 20, 23

Opening times
Mon.–Sat. 9 a.m.–noon

St Peter in Gallicantu   F8

The Church of St Peter in Gallicantu (at the cock's crow), consecrated in 1931, stands on the E slope of Mount Zion (see entry), on the path from Coenaculum to the Pool of Siloah (see Kidron Valley). Roman steps lead down the steep slope and some sections of them can still be used.

In 457 a church in memory of St Peter was built here. After its destruction it was rebuilt by the Crusaders in 1010 and then destroyed again in 1320. Excavations were begun in 1888 which uncovered Jewish weights, a Hebrew inscription, the Roman steps mentioned above, cisterns of the Herodian period and other important finds.

Location
Malki Zedeq

Bus
1, 38 (Wailing Wall)

Opening times
Mon.–Sat. 8.30–11.30 a.m.,
2–5 p.m.

The modern, present-day church stands on foundations of the Herodian and early Christian period, according to tradition on the spot where Caiaphas' palace once stood. There is a grotto here which is thought to be the place where Jesus was detained by the High Priests (Christ's Prison). Excavations have shown, however, that at the time of Caiaphas there must have been a cemetery here.

The name of the church refers to the story of Peter in Caiaphas' palace, where he thrice denied Christ. Prior to this Jesus had told Peter: "Before the cock crows, you will have denied me thrice" (Matthew 26:75).

The church belongs to the Assumptionists, a Catholic Augustine congregation.

St Stephen

D7/8

Location
Derekh Shekhem

Buses
12, 27

The Dominican church of St Stephen stands at the centre of a large complex of buildings on the Derekh Shekhem not far from the Damascus Gate (see entry). As well as the church and the Dominican monastery, the French Institute for Biblical Archaeology is also situated here.

The present-day church – its crypt is dedicated to St Stephen – was erected between 1883 and 1900 on the ruins of a 5th c. basilica.

The plan of the Byzantine building was closely followed. The floor is decorated with 5th c. mosaics.

In 460 Eudocia, wife of Emperor Theodosius II, built a basilica with nave and side aisles to house the bones of Stephen, the first martyr, found in 417. After the destruction of the basilica by the Persians (614) a small chapel was built which the Crusaders extended but then tore down in the face of Saladin's imminent conquest of Jerusalem (1187).

The remains of 5th c. plaster and a cistern are preserved in the atrium. In the N part there are rock-cut tombs bearing Greek inscriptions.

Ecole Biblique et
Archéologique Française

The French Institute for Biblical Archaeology houses a huge library and a museum with finds from the 1883 excavations. The most important exhibits are the remains of the Byzantine basilica and Crusader chapel.

Sanhedrin Tombs

B6

Location
Sanhedriya

Bus
2

Opening times
Tombs: Sun.–Fri. 9 a.m.–6 p.m.
Park: Sun.–Sat. 9 a.m.–6 p.m.

In the northernmost part of the modern North-City lie the rock-cut tombs of members of the High Council (Sanhedrin). Synhedrium is the greek name for the highest ranking judges up until Herod the Great (to 37 B.C.). Later, the Romans reserved jurisdiction in the Criminal Courts for themselves but right up until its disbandment in A.D. 70 the Synhedrium remained the highest religious court for the Jews. Today this function has been taken over by the Chief Rabbinate.

The rock-cut tombs, principally in use in the 1st c. A.D., possess a multitude of grave recesses. At the entrance lie the boulders which closed the tombs. The walls bear incised decoration in the form of acanthus leaves, pomegranates and lemons.

The Keren Kajemeth Leismael (Jewish National Fund) set up a
camp site not far from these tombs. Here water, shade
(important in summer), a post office, benches and tables are
provided. You can plant a tree here yourself and festive tree-
planting sessions take place; especially during the "Festival of
the Trees" (January/February).

Shechem

See Nablus

Solomon's Pools

In a grove of palm and fir trees 2 miles/3 km S of Bethlehem   **Location**
(see entry) lie what are known as Solomon's Pools. These are   10 miles/16 km S
three reservoirs set on different levels and fed by rainwater,
springs and by aqueducts. The foundations of the first reservoir
(380 ft/116 m × 230 ft/70 m × 23 ft/7 m) date from the time
when work commenced on the Second Temple (6th c. B.C.).
Jerusalem was supplied with water via aqueducts. The upper
aqueduct was built by Herod and was also intended to supply
the fortress of Herodion (see entry).
The beauty of the countryside and the abundant vegetation
have made the place very popular for excursions.

Stephen's Gate

See Lion Gate

Sultan's Pool (Birket Sultan)   F7

The Sultan's Pool, 558 ft/170 m long and 220 ft/67 m wide, was   **Location**
created by damming. It lies between Mount Zion (see entry) and   Hativat Yerushaliyim
the Yemin Moshe part of town. Although still forming part of the
water supply of the Old Town, it was probably first constructed   **Buses**
during the period of the Jewish kings.   13, 19, 20, 23 (Jaffa Gate)
The name "Sultan's Pool" refers to Sultan Suleiman the
Magnificent who undertook repairs here while building the
wall around the Old Town (1537–40).
The recently built Merrill Hassenfeld Amphitheatre was   Amphitheatre
inaugurated in 1981.

Terra Sancta College   E6

One of the buildings belonging to the Terra Sancta College is   **Location**
the Terra Sancta Church founded in 1927. Its statue of Mary   Balfour
can be seen from far off. Services are held here daily at 7 a.m.   Corner of Keren Ha-Yessod
(Latin), 10.30 a.m. (French) and 6.30 p.m. (English).
In 1929 the Franciscans took over the grounds and erected   **Buses**
further buildings. Between 1948 and 1967, when teaching in   4, 7, 9, 10, 16, 17, 19
the Hebrew University on Mount Scopus was virtually at a
standstill, the Terra Sancta College offered temporary accommodation to some of the institutes.

Tomb of the Holy Virgin

See Mount of Olives

Tomb of Rachel

See Bethlehem

*Tombs of the Kings   C7

Location
Derekh Shekhem

Buses
12, 27

Opening times
Daily 8.30 a.m.–5 p.m.

The Tombs of the Kings are among the most interesting burial sites in Israel This impressive necropolis was long thought to be the burial site of the Jewish kings, hence the name: "Tombs of the Kings". In fact it was Queen "Helena" of Adiabene (Mesopotamia) who originally had these tombs cut into the rock. The queen – called "Helena" by the Greeks – came to Jerusalem in A.D. 45 and was converted to Judaism.

26 wide steps cut into the rock lead down to a practically square courtyard (91 ft/28 m long, 84 ft/26 m wide), which lies 26 ft/8 m below street level. There are cisterns at the base of the steps to catch any rainwater.

The ante-chamber is reached through a low entrance (height 2½ ft/80 cm) and the rock-cut tombs, once sealed by boulders, can be reached from here. The tombs are decorated with ancient fertility symbols: vine leaves, pine cones, acanthus, floral wreathes, etc.

Tombs of the Kings: one of Israel's most impressive necropoli

In 1863 the richly decorated sarcophagus of the queen was discovered in a secret chamber. Today it is in the Louvre in Paris. The sarcophagi of the other tombs, however, lacking the security of a secret passage, have been looted by grave-robbers.

**Via Dolorosa

D/E8

Via Dolorosa, the "Street of Sorrows", can be either the name given to the 14 Stations of the Cross or to a narrow, oriental bazaar street which begins in the Moslem quarter of the Old Town and ends in the Church of the Holy Sepulchre (see entry) in the Christian quarter.

The route followed by the street, Via Dolorosa, and the route of the Stations of the Cross are not the same, because the Stations of the Cross are based on religious belief rather than on the facts of archaeological evidence. Accordingly the route has often been changed over the centuries and the original seven stations have grown over the years to 14. Most of the present route dates from the 18th c. Stations I, IV, V and VIII were only decided upon in the 19th c.

This short explanation should suffice to make the distinction. For those who make their pilgrimage on foot down these narrow streets, sharing the final stages of Christ's passion, it is not the historical facts that are of importance so much as the feeling imparted by the ancient walls and stones.

Location
Old Town

Buses
2, 12, 27

Procession
Fri. 3 p.m. Starting from Station I (Courtyard of El Omariye School)

Via Dolorosa: Ecce Homo Arch

"The Cross is brought to Jesus"

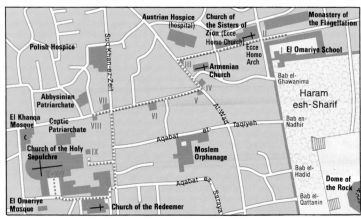

Via Dolorosa I . . . XIV Fourteen Stations of the Cross

I   Jesus is condemned to death by crucifixion by Pontius Pilate
II Jesus takes up the Cross
III Jesus falls for the first time
IV Jesus meets his mother
V   Simon of Cyrene helps Jesus to carry the Cross
VI Veronica hands Jesus the handkerchief
VII Jesus falls for the second time
VIII Jesus comforts the women of Jerusalem
IX Jesus falls for the third time

IN THE CHURCH OF THE HOLY SEPULCHRE
X   Jesus is disrobed
XI   Jesus is crucified
XII Jesus dies on the Cross
XIII Jesus' body is taken down from the Cross
XIV Jesus' body is laid in the tomb (Holy Sepulchre)

Golgotha

Route of Procession

Antonia Fortress

The Via Dolorosa begins to the N of the Temple precinct (Haram esh-Sharif, see entry) in the area formerly occupied by the Antonia fortress. This fortress, of which there are only few remains, was named by Herod the Great after his friend and patron Mark Antony, the Roman triumvir who committed suicide in Alexandria with Cleopatra in 30 B.C. After the death of Herod, the fortress was used as the official residence of the Roman governor, as quarters for the garrison and as a prison. There is lively discussion about the exact siting of each part. The Stations from the El Omariye School to the Ecce Homo Church may have been within the area of the Antonia fortress.

El Omariye School

Steps lead from the street into the courtyard of the El Omariye School (admittance only on Fridays, Moslem holidays and during the lunch break). All of Haram esh-Sharif (see entry) can be seen from here, and the watch towers of the Antonia fortress probably stood here. Any suspicious gatherings on the Temple Square, known to be a trouble spot, could be noted immediately and broken up by the troops.

Station I

Station I of the Via Dolorosa is in the courtyard of the El Omariye School. It is, however, uncertain whether the praetorium in which Jesus was condemned really stood here. On the Feast of the Passover the Roman governor used to set a Jewish prisoner free. Mark says that the Jewish people "went up" (15:8) when Pilate allowed them to choose between Jesus and the "Robber", that is the anti-Roman resistance fighter and terrorist, Barabbas. Influenced by the campaigns of harassment arranged by the chief priests opposed to Jesus, the crowd chose Barabbas. Pilate washed his hands of the responsibility "and all the people answered and said, His blood be on us and on our children" (Matthew 27:25).

Mark's quotation is taken to mean that Jesus must have been condemned on a high place. The words "Gabbatha" and "Lithostrotos" mean "Pavement of Justice" and "High Pavement". Since El Omariye School is sufficiently high to be able to overlook the place where the Temple Square used to lie, this is probably seen as Station I.

Station II lies at the other side of the road from the El Omariye School. According to tradition, Jesus took up the cross here.

Station II

Chapels of Flagellation and Judgement
On the right of Station II stands the Chapel of Flagellation and on the left the Chapel of Judgement. Both chapels belong to the Franciscans. Stones from the Pavement of Justice are on display in the chapel of Judgement (see below, Ecce Homo Church).

Ecce Homo Arch
A little further in the direction of Station III the Ecce Homo Arch spans the Via Dolorosa. It was supposedly under this arch that Pilate said "Ecce Homo" ("Behold the man"; John 19:5) when he presented Jesus to the crowd after his flagellation, dressed, as a mocking gesture, in kingly garb and wearing a crown of thorns.

Street sign for the Via Dolorosa

141

The arch has only had this name since the 16th c. and is part of a gate dating from the time of Hadrian (2nd c. A.D.).

Ecce Homo Church
The church of the French sisters of Zion was called the Ecce Homo Church after the arch of that name. Further fragments of the hadrianic gate are displayed here, as are larger pieces of the Pavement of Justice or High Pavement (Hebrew: Gabbatha; Greek: Lithostrotos; John 19:13) on which Pilate's seat of judgement stood.
These are roughly cut paving stones in which channels or runnels have been set at regular intervals so that the rainwater could be channelled off into subterranean cisterns. There is such a cistern under the church.
The designs incised on the paving stones are also of interest (squares, triangles, a crown, etc.). They can be traced back to the board games played by the Roman sentries.
The church is now open Monday–Saturday from 8 a.m. to noon and 2.30 to 6 p.m. The Sisters of Zion provide detailed guided tours.

Station III

Station III of the Cross is in remembrance of Jesus falling for the first time under the weight of the Cross.

Station IV

A relief on the arch over the entrance to the Armenian church commemorates Station IV when Jesus met his mother. In the crypt of the Armenian church are the prints of two sandals which symbolise the place where Mary stood as she watched her son go past on the way to his crucifixion.

Station V

"The Cross is given to Simon of Cyrene"
As the troop with the three condemned men was leaving the town a North African labourer was forced to carry the Cross (Simon of Cyrene probably carried the long bar).
As you turn from King Solomon Street (Ha Gay or El Wad) into the Via Dolorosa you see a hand print on the first house on the left. According to tradition this is the print left by Christ's hand as he leant against the wall.

Station VI

It was at Station VI that St Veronica is said to have offered Jesus her handkerchief.
A (very recent) version of the popular legend says that Veronica wanted a portrait of Christ so that she might at least always have a picture of her Lord before her. On the way she met Jesus and told him of her intentions. Jesus asked for her handkerchief, laid it on his face, and when he gave it back to Veronica the sweat had left an imprint of the Lord's face on it. Veronica is supposed to have gone to Emperor Tiberias (A.D. 14–37) with the sudarium to make accusations against Pilate. When the emperor saw the picture he was cured of an illness and had Pilate brought before the courts. St Veronica's handkerchief is today kept in St Peter's in Rome.
An "authentic" picture of the face of Christ, that is, one not painted by human hand, is known as a Vera Ikon (true picture). The name Veronica could be a corruption of Vera Ikon.

Station VII

Station VII marks the place where Jesus fell for the second time. At this spot the Via Dolorosa starts to go uphill.

Station VIII

After crossing the bazaar street Suq Khan ez-Zeit you come to

Station VIII which is marked with a cross and the Greek inscription NIKA.
It was here that Jesus is said to have told the lamenting "Daughters of Jerusalem" to weep rather for themselves and their children than for him, for the day would come when they would say: "Blessed are the barren, and the wombs that never bare, and the breasts that never gave suck. Then shall they begin to say to the mountains, Fall on us; and to the hills, cover us" (Luke 23:29–30).

A flight of 28 stone steps leads up from the bazaar street to the entrance of the Coptic Patriarchate. Station IX, where Jesus stumbled for the third time under the Cross, is at the gate. From here you can see over to the "Roof-top Monastery" of the Ethiopian Abyssinians. **Station IX**
Since access to the Church of the Holy Sepulchre (see entry) across the area of the Abyssinians is forbidden, the route now doubles back to the bazaar street around the Russian Orthodox Alexander Hospice (see entry) opposite which stands the Church of the Redeemer. Entering a small door one comes to the atrium of the Church of the Holy Sepulchre, in which Stations X to XIV are situated (see Church of the Holy Sepulchre: Golgotha and Tomb).

Every Friday there is a procession led by the Franciscans. It starts from Station I at 3 p.m. Anyone may take part in the procession which visits all the Stations of the Cross. **Advice**

Visitatio Maria (Church)

See En Karem

---

*Wailing Wall and excavations (officially: Western Wall) E8

The Wailing Wall (Western Wall) is the holiest site in Jewry. As the only remaining part of the Second Temple it both symbolises the Temple itself and commemorates its destruction.
For centuries Jews living in dispersement (Diaspora) came to this wall to lament and to pray.
Under some rulers they even had to pay a fee to come here, at other times they were forbidden to come here at all.
Today the laments are fewer, but it is still said that the dew which settles on the stones overnight is the tears that have flowed here.
Up until 1967 houses were built right up against the wall. After the annexing of East Jerusalem and the reuniting of the town during the Six Day War all the houses were pulled down and a wide square created. Religious and national ceremonies take place here, such as those in remembrance of the destruction of the Temple (usually in August), the festival of the Ark of the Covenant at the end of the Feast of the Tabernacle (September to October), also the swearing in of parachutists (they recaptured the wall in 1967).
Following the Six Day War the wall was given the official title "Western Wall" since it formed part of the western boundary of

Location
Jewish Old Town

Bus
1, 38

Wailing Wall

The Wailing Wall (Western Wall): holiest site in Jewry

Supplications on paper slips in the cracks in the Wailing Wall

A solitary supplicant by the huge stone blocks of the Wailing Wall ▶

Haram esh-Sharif (see entry), the Temple precinct, and it was considered undesirable to give it a name which would continue to invoke the tragic past.

The Jews come here to pray or to write their requests on scraps of paper which are pushed into cracks in the wall so that their supplications are put directly before the Lord. The areas for prayer are divided off by railings: the one on the right is for women (smaller area), the one on the left is for men.

The wall reaches a height of 58 ft/18 m and is constructed of courses of stones from very different periods. The massive limestone blocks from Herodian times (lower five courses) are of such huge size that the heads of supplicants barely reach the second course. Overlying these are four courses of stone from the Roman period, while the upper courses are of Moslem date – in part 19th c. There are 19 subterranean courses (the basal layer lying on bedrock).

To the N and more especially to the S of the Wailing Wall the features uncovered by excavation, some dating to the pre-Herodian period (up to c. 30 B.C.), are open to the public.

Tunnel to the Wilson Arch

Opening times
Sun., Tues., Wed. 8.30 a.m.–3 p.m., Mon., Thurs. 12.30–3 p.m., closed Sat.

The entrance tunnel into the N area of excavation also provides access from the Old Town (Haggai Street) into Haram esh-Sharif (see entry) and to the Wailing Wall. The tunnel was opened to the public after the Six Day War. It is made up of several vaulted areas with arches. The N part is dated to the 15th/16th c. The central arch is the oldest and possibly belongs to the time of the Second Temple.

Looking down through a lattice window one can see into a pre-Herodian room. Beneath the entrance lies a Roman-Byzantine street. The tunnel and street were probably still in use at the time of the Crusades and were subsequently blocked up with rubble.

The last and greatest arch, the Wilson Arch, named after the archaeologist C. Wilson who discovered it, dates from the 7th/8th c. but also exhibits some Herodian elements (columns).

Southern Area of Excavation

In the excavated area S of the Wailing Wall the features and structures from Herodian and Omayyaden times are open to the public: a street laid by Herod, a bath house and two inns (with gates) from the time of the Omayyads, remains of Byzantine houses, some of them with mosaic floors.

Here the double portal on the S wall of Haram esh-Sharif (see entry) is to be found.

Double Portal

The double portal is in the S wall of Haram esh-Sharif (see entry) below the El Aqsa Mosque. It forms one of the entrances to Herod's Temple. Some of the steps have been replaced, but the older ones date from the time of Herod. Stucco-work and mouldings are attributed to the Omayyaden period. Many of the elements of the double portal are reminiscent of the Golden Gate (see Haram esh-Sharif) on the E wall. Both gates were probably replaced at the same time (early Byzantine, 5th/6th c.).

Also in the S wall is the triple portal. In the area in front of it can be seen the walls of an Omayyaden building and of a Herodian palace. The wall of Empress Eudocia (post A.D. 444) leads off from the SE corner of Haram esh-Sharif (see entry) to a tomb and the remains of an 8th c. tower.

Western Wall

See Wailing Wall

Yad Vashem (Memorial)

E1

On Har Hazikkaron, the mountain of remembrance and commemoration, the Yad Vashem Memorial was set up by the State of Israel to commemorate the six million Jews murdered by the Nazis from 1933 to 1945.

The central archives of Yad Vashem contain a comprehensive collection of documents and a large library of books from the Hitler regime. The largest collection of antisemitic literature in the world is housed here, including neo-Nazi newpapers and magazines.

The Yad Vashem Memorial maintains contact with many other institutes all over the world which research the Nazi regime.

Location
Har Hazikkaron (near Mount Herzl)

Buses
5, 6, 12, 13, 18, 20, 21, 23, 24, 26, 27, 33 (to Mount Herzl)

Opening times
Sun.–Thurs. 9 a.m.–4.45 p.m., Fri. 9 a.m.–12.45 p.m.
Museum: Sun.–Thurs. 9 a.m.–5 p.m., Fri. 9 a.m.–2 p.m.

Yad Vashem: Memorial to the victims of the Nazis

Yad Vashem

Ohel Jiskor

The Ohel Jiskor is a hall dedicated to the memory of the dead. It is a square building with a tent-shaped roof (Ohel = tent). The concrete walls rest on blocks of basalt.

The names of 21 Nazi extermination camps have been chiselled into the huge stone flags on the floor: Maidanek, Buchenwald, Bergen-Belsen, Auschwitz, etc. Every day at 11 a.m. candles are lit in memory of the dead.

In June 1981 about 5000 survivors of Nazi extermination camps met in Jerusalem and on their first day they assembled in the Ohel Jiskor. The travellers had come from 27 different countries and they carried stones in their hands; on each stone was scratched the name of a murdered relative. These stones have been heaped on Yad Vashem to form a monument.

Exhibition

The permanent exhibition "Warning and Witness" shows the horror of the Nazi period. The documents and photographs, newspaper cuttings and pamphlets, etc., make a forceful impression on the visitor.

Wall of Holocaust and Heroism

The Wall of Holocaust and Heroism is the work of Naftali Bezem. Bezem was born in Essen, West Germany, in 1924 but managed to emigrate in time.

The wall is a flat relief cast in aluminium which stretches over a black surface 72 sq. yd/60 sq. m in size and consists of four parts: the first part symbolises extermination in the form of an industrial plant with cremation furnaces. A fish's body with detached head represents "muteness". Angels' wings accompany the fish to heaven.

The second part of the relief shows the "resistance": houses go up in flames, a hand holds a weapon while the other holds a ladder as the symbol of climbing upwards and of hope.

The third part symbolises the return to the land of Israel. An armed man stands prepared to disembark from a boat guided by angels' wings.

The fourth part shows the "rebirth": although the lion is the epitome of strength and might, he sheds tears at the thought of the terrors and atrocities of the past. A plant with cactus leaves symbolises the generation following the Holocaust.

Hall of Names

The names of over two million Jews who were murdered during the Nazi regime are recorded in the Hall of Names. The details come from the relatives of the deceased.

Many families were wiped out so entirely, however, that there was no one left to enter their names in the register.

Janusz Korczak Park

A park was created in memory of the murder of so many Jewish children. It bears the name of the famous Polish pedagogue, Janusz Korczak. Korczak went voluntarily with children into the extermination camp at Treblinka. A tall column in the park serves as a memorial. Sculptures serve as poignant reminders of the horrors of the past.

The Way of the Righteous

The Way of the Righteous was constructed in honour of those who helped Jews at the risk of their own lives during the Nazi regime.

A plaque bearing the name and nationality of each "righteous" person stands by every tree.

Valley of the Communities — new in 95.

The modern buildings of the Y.M.C.A.

Y.M.C.A.   E6/7

The design of the Y.M.C.A. (Young Men's Christian Association), opened in 1933, was the work of A. L. Harmon, the architect of the New York State Building. It has a tower 150 ft/46 m high; an indoor swimming pool; a library; reading rooms; halls for cultural functions; accommodation and the Clarck "Collection of Near Eastern Antiquities".

There are extensive panoramic views from the top of the tower (there is a charge for the lift). A carillon is played here on public holidays and on special occasions.

The Y.M.C.A. football stadium is situated next to the building together with athletic grounds, tennis courts and other sports facilities.

Location
David Ha Melekh

Buses
6, 15, 18   *across the street from King David Hotel.*

Opening times
Tower: Mon.–Fri.
9 a.m.–3 p.m., Sat.
9 a.m.–1 p.m.

Zedekiah's Cave   D8

Zedekiah's Cave, extending almost 650 ft/200 m under the Old Town, was discovered in the mid 19th c. Jewish tradition sees it as part of the route taken by King Zedekiah (597–587 B.C.) in his flight from the Babylonians (Jeremiah 52:7 et seq.).

The most interesting aspect of the caves, however, is the traces of ancient quarrying. Grooves were chased into the rock defining the outline of the stone block required. Wedges of dry wood were then hammered into the grooves and soaked with water. The wedges increased in volume as they soaked up the water and so cracked the stone.

Location
Sultan Suleiman Road
(between Damascus Gate
and Herod's Gate)

Buses
2, 12

Opening times
Sun.–Thurs. 8 a.m.–4 p.m.,
Fri. 8 a.m.–1 p.m.

149

For the building of the First Temple King Solomon had 80,000 men trained as masons (1 Kings 5:29 et seq.) and it is assumed that the stones for Solomon's Temple were quarried in this cave. For this reason Zedekiah's Cave is also known as "Solomon's Quarry".

Freemasons used to hold their meetings here and the signs of lodges scratched on the rocks bear witness to these secret gatherings.

Zion Gate   F7/8

Location
'Ezyyoni

Bus
1

Opening times
Wall: Sun.–Thurs.
9 a.m.–9.30 p.m., Fri. 9 a.m.–
3 p.m.

The Zion Gate leads from the SW part of the Old Town to Mount Zion. As with most of the other gates to the Old Town, this too was constructed during the building of the wall in the time of Sultan Suleiman the Magnificent. It was, however, one of the last to be completed (an inscription gives the date as 1540).

Sultan Suleiman had originally ordered that Mount Zion and the Coenaculum should be included within the walls and when the plan failed owing to lack of funds, it is said that Suleiman hanged the architects.

Between 1948 and 1967 the Zion Gate stood on the border between the Israeli Mount Zion and the Jordan occupied Old Town. Evidence of frequent exchanges of fire is still visible today.

Practical Information

Advance booking

Advance booking offices for the theatre and all other cultural
activities:
Ben Naim, 38 Yafo, tel. 22 40 08
Cahana, 12 Shammay, tel. 22 28 31
Cartis On, 8 Shammay, tel. 22 46 24
Kla'im, 8 Shammay, tel. 24 08 96

Airlines

Air France
King David Hotel extension, tel. 22 29 45

Alitalia
23 Rechov Hillel, tel. 22 86 53

Arkia (domestic airline)
9 Heleni Ha-Malka, tel. 22 58 88

British Airways
33 Yafo Road (Bet Yoel), tel. 23 31 11

El Al
12 Rechov Hillel, tel. 26 67 25

KLM
33 Yafo Road (Bet Yoel), tel. 22 13 61

Olympic Airways
33 Yafo Road (Bet Yoel), tel. 23 45 38

Sabena
King David Hotel extension, tel. 23 49 71

SAS
Az-Zahara, tel. 28 32 35

Supercharter-Galilee Tours
3 Ben Sira Street, tel. 24 27 20, 24 61 41

Swissair
30 Yafo Road, tel. 22 52 33

TWA
Ha-Melekh George, multi-storey building, 5th floor,
tel. 24 11 35/6

PanAm
By prior appointment only, tel. 63 17 40

Varing
33 Yafo Road (Bet Yoel), tel. 22 55 23

I.S.S.T.A. (student flights)
5 Elayazhor Street, tel. 23 14 18

Airports

Ben Gurion

Ben Gurion international airport at Lod is about 18 miles/30 km NW of Jerusalem on the road to Tel Aviv, tel. (03) 97 14 85/7.

Arrival

The airport operates the red and green channel system for passengers passing through customs. All items subject to duty (see Customs regulations) must be declared on entry even if they may be temporarily imported free of duty. Passengers bringing such items should take the red channel.

Transfer to Jerusalem

El Al airport bus
The El Al airport bus leaves Ben Gurion airport for Jerusalem every hour on the hour from 6 a.m. to 10 p.m. Extra buses operate during peak hours. The journey takes about 45 minutes.

Egged bus
Between 7.45 a.m. and 6.45 p.m. Egged buses leave for Jerusalem every 45 minutes. The journey takes just under an hour. Egged Tours also provide bus connections to the major Jerusalem hotels.

Sherut taxis
Sherut taxis (see Taxis) are slightly more expensive than the buses but they do the trip from Lod to Jerusalem in well under an hour.

There is an official farescale which passengers should be able to see.

Departure

It is advisable to confirm bookings and the times of flights at least 72 hours before take-off. It takes at least two hours to check in. El Al passengers can check in their baggage on the eve of departure at the El Al air terminal offices (closed on Fridays and the evenings before a public holiday), it is then only necessary to check in at the airport an hour before departure. An airport charge is levied for departing flights. Further information is available when making flight bookings or reservations.

Transfer to Ben Gurion airport

Egged buses
Egged buses leave Jerusalem for Ben Gurion airport approximately every 45 minutes from 6.15 a.m. to 7 p.m. There are pick-up services for the larger hotels.

Nesher Sherut taxis
Sherut taxis for Ben Gurion airport should be booked in advance:
21 Ha-Melekh George, tel. 22 72 27.

Atarot airport for internal flights

Internal flights for Tel Aviv, Haifa, Rosh Pinna, Eilat and Ofira leave from Atarot airport which is about 6 miles/10 km N of Jerusalem.

Antiques

For the Israeli, archaeology, particularly where it concerns biblical history, has become something of a national pastime. It comes as no surprise that the shopkeepers want to cash in on this. Most of the so-called "antiques" are downright fakes and it is advisable to shop where you see the seal of government approval, depicting two figures carrying a large bunch of grapes. This signifies that the goods on sale – including the antiques – are of reasonably high quality.

Some addresses:
Antique Shop, David Street
Iran Bazaar, 3 Ben Yehuda
Israeli Souvenirs, 53 Jaffa Road
Sasson Antiques, David Ha-Melekh, in the King David Hotel
Via Dolorosa Souvenir Shop, 60 Via Dolorosa

Written permission is required for the export of antiques dating from before 1700 (export fee).   Export

Banks

The majority of Jerusalem's many banks are located in the city centre streets of Yafo, Ben Yehuda, Ha-Melekh George and Hillel. All banks will change foreign currency, traveller's cheques and Israel Bonds. Eurocheques are accepted in all branches of the larger banks.

Bank of Israel, 29 Yafo Road, Mitzpeh Building   Some addresses
Bank Leumi, 21 Yafo Road
Foreign Trade Bank, 6 Hillel Road and 27 Gaza Road
Tefahot, 9 Heleni Ha-Malka
United Mizrahi Bank, 5 Ben Yehuda

Some banks have branches in the larger hotels.

Sun., Mon., Tues., Thurs. 8.30 a.m.–12.30 p.m., 4–5 or   Opening times
5.30 p.m., Wed. 8.30 a.m.–12.30 p.m., Fri. 8.30 a.m.–noon.

Calendar of events

The following dates are only approximate because the Jewish and Moslem calendars are based on the moon and many of the Christian festivals have no fixed date.

Jewish: January/February
Tu Be Shevat: 15th Shevat.
Tu Be Shevat means the "feast of the trees" and celebrates the coming of spring. It used to be the day when the Jews had to pay their tithes in fruit from the trees. On this occasion the Jews eat 15 different kinds of fruit. Tree-planting ceremonies take place everywhere, particularly in the John F. Kennedy peace forest, in the Tree-Planting Centre near the Sanhedrin Graves (see A–Z, Sanhedrin Graves) and in the Forest of the Martyrs in the Judean Hills. Anyone can plant a tree with their own hands and obtain a certificate for doing so.

153

Practical Information

<table>
<tr><td>February/March</td><td>

Jewish:
Purim: 14th Adar.
Purim, the festival of Queen Esther, commemorates the deliverance of the Persian Jews from the massacre planned by Haman. The Book of Esther in the Old Testament tells how Esther, the Jewish wife of the Persian ruler Xerxes I, made herself known to her people and thus thwarted Haman's plans. Theatre performances are put on in Yiddish, particularly in the Ashkenazi (European Jewish) communities These are usually one-act burlesques with a biblical theme. There are street parades, children in fancy dress, dancing, singing and the exchange of presents.

</td></tr>
<tr><td>March/April</td><td>

Jewish:
Pesach (Passover): 15th Nisan.
Pesach commemorates the night before the exodus of the Israelites from Egypt (see Introduction, History of Jerusalem). Pesach is also called "the feast of the unleavened bread", because of the unleavened bread eaten in the Pesach week as a reminder of the haste with which the Israelites had to leave Egypt. Everything eaten or drunk during Pesach week has a symbolic significance. The saltwater stands for the tears the Israelites shed during the Egyptian bondage. The period between Pesach and Shavuot – 50 days altogether – is one of mourning.

Christian:
Palm Sunday: the Sunday before Easter.
Palm Sunday, the last Sunday before Easter week, commemorates Christ's entry into Jerusalem. A magnificent procession wends its way from the village of Bethphage on the Mount of Olives to the Church of the Holy Sepulchre (see A–Z, Mount of Olives, Bethphage).

Easter
At Easter Christians commemorate Christ's Resurrection. Since the Christian sects are unable to agree on the precise day of the Resurrection it is celebrated on different days. The most spectacular of the Easter celebrations "Appearance of the Holy Fire" is the Armenian/Greek Orthodox (see A–Z, Church of the Holy Sepulchre, Holy Tomb).

Moslem:
Maulid.
As the birthday of Mohammed, Maulid is a popular Moslem festival, usually celebrated by public readings of prize-winning Maulid poetry.

Non-religious:
Israeli Spring Festival, celebrated in April.
This is the occasion for a festival of music, theatre and dance in the Jerusalem theatre on Chopin Street.
International Book Fair (April).

</td></tr>
<tr><td>April/May</td><td>

Jewish:
Independence Day: 5th Iyar.

Lag Ba'Omer: 18th Iyar.
Lag Ba'Omer (lag=33) is celebrated on the 33rd day after Pesach and interrupts the period of mourning between Pesach and Shavuot for half a day. It is said that during a 1st c. epidemic none of the sick died on the 33rd day of this epidemic.

</td></tr>
</table>

Christian:
Ascension Day: the 40th day after Easter.
There is a church service from midnight until noon in the courtyard of the Chapel of the Ascension on the Mount of Olives (see A–Z, Mount of Olives, Ascension Chapel).

Non-religious:
14th May: Independence Day; Jerusalem Day: 28th Iyar.

Jewish: May/June
Shavuot: 50th day after Pesach.
Shavuot is a kind of harvest festival to conclude the 50 days of mourning after Pesach. There are readings from the Old Testament Book of Ruth (see A–Z, Bethlehem, Field of Ruth).

Jewish: July/August
Tisha B'ay: 9th Av.
Tisha B'ay is a day of mourning and fasting to commemorate the destruction of the temples in 587 B.C. and A.D. 70. There are readings on this day from the laments in the Old Testament Books of Job and Jeremiah.

Non-religious:
Israel Festival.

Jewish: September/October
Rosh Hashana: 1st and 2nd Tishri.
This is the first day of the Jewish calendar year. It is also the first of the ten days of fasting at the beginning of this year. Over these ten days one hears all around the sound of the Shofar, the curved ram's horn, calling the listener to fasting and contemplation. Many Jews wear white clothes as a sign of the transitory nature of man and their trust in God. The Tashlih ceremoney is held at the Pool of Siloah (see A–Z, Mount of Olives) when sins are symbolically cast into the water.

Yom Kippur: 10th Tishri.
Yom Kippur is the most important of the Jewish festivals. It is the last of the ten days of fasting at the beginning of the Jewish calendar year and dates back to the Day of Atonement laid down by Moses (Moses 3:16).

Sukkoth: 15th–21st Tishri.
During the seven days of Sukkoth which is a kind of general harvest festival the Jews build little huts in their gardens, courtyards, on balconies, etc., where they take their meals and, if they are orthodox, sleep at night. In Israel only the first of the seven days of Sukkoth is a public holiday.

Simhath Torah: 22nd Tishri.
The feast of rejoicing over the Law (the Torah) marks the end of Sukkoth. The Torah is carried in procession all around the city.

Moslem: October/November
Ramadan, the ninth month of the Islamic calendar year, is the Moslem month of fasting. From dawn to dusk Moslems may not eat, drink or smoke. This is relaxed during the hours of darkness.

Practical Information

Lailat al Kadr, the "night of the Divine Power", is celebrated on the night of the 26th day of Ramadan, in commemoration of the night that the Koran was handed down to mankind.

Camp sites

All of Israel's 16 State camp sites have electricity, places to eat and/or shop, telephones and washing, postal, first-aid and leisure facilities. There are swimming facilities at almost all of them. Tents, cabins and camping equipment can be hired on site.

The 14-day card is recommended. This covers accommodation (tent, cabin, or caravan fitted out with bedding) at one of the sites (with the possibility of a transfer), continental breakfast and the bus fare from one site to another.

Information

Details are available from the Israel Camping Union. A brochure can be obtained from any Israel Government Tourist Office (see Information).

Camp site near Jerusalem

En Hemed (Aqua Bella near Beth Negofa) 7 miles/11 km W.

Car hire

Nearly all the international car hire firms have branches in Jerusalem and at Ben Gurion airport (see Airports).

Documents

A national driving licence suffices for a stay of up to 1 year in Israel. For a longer stay an international driving licence is required.

Chemists

Alba Pharmacy, 42 Yafo Road (Kikkar Ziyyon).

Opening times

Sun.–Thurs. 8.30 a.m.–1 p.m., 4–7 p.m., Fri. 9.30 a.m.–2 p.m.

Night service

The list of chemists open at night can be found in the daily newspapers; it is also available in every hotel and from Magen David Adom.

Emergency service

Magen David Adom ("Red Star of David")
Ha-Mem Gimmel (Romema district), tel. 101.

Churches

The times given are for Sunday Services in English:

Catholic (selection)

Ecce Homo Church (Sisters of Zion)
Via Dolorosa
6 p.m.

Gethsemane (Basilica)
11.30 a.m.

St George's Cathedral
Nablus Road
8, 11 a.m., 6 p.m.

Christ Church
Jaffa Gate
8, 11 a.m., 6.45 p.m.

Baptist Tourist Chapel
6 Rasheed Street
11 a.m.

Church of Nazarene (international)
33 Nablus Road
11 a.m., 6 p.m.

Garden Tomb (Inter-Denominational)
Nablus Road
9 a.m.

Scottish Church of St Andrew
Aarekevet Street
10 a.m.

Protestant (selection)

Cinemas

Jerusalem's 20 or so cinemas also show a number of foreign films. All films are screened in the original version with Modern Hebrew, English or French subtitles. There are usually two evening performances and one in the afternoon.

Climate

Israel's Mediterranean climate, with its extreme heat and very low humidity, is more agreeable in Jerusalem because it lies in the hilly country. Spring and autumn are very short, with most of the year taken up by the summer and winter.
During the summer season (April–October) the August temperature can climb well into the 90s (over 30 °C). It is much cooler by contrast, in the evening and at night and the air is relatively dry.
During the winter season (November–March) temperatures can fall as low as 40 °F (6 °C), despite the generally mild climate. Frequent rainfall in winter can turn to snow.
In the winter the ideal climate for Europeans is by the Dead Sea which, even in January, can boast of water temperatures of 70 °F (21 °C) (see When to go).

Clothing

Visitors to Israel should be prepared for any kind of weather at any time of year. Snow may be falling in Jerusalem while tropical fruit-trees are blooming in Jericho 28 miles/35 km to the NE and holidaymakers are sunbathing by the Dead Sea.

In the summer it is advisable to wear light clothing, headgear and sun-glasses during the day. Footwear should have thick rubber soles because of the state of the streets, etc. Because of the mountains the evenings in Jerusalem can be very chilly, so it is useful to take a pullover even in the summer.

When considering what to wear tourists should not forget that they are visitors in a foreign land in a city which is a holy place for Jews, Christians and Moslems. The religious sensitivity of all believers should be respected. In the orthodox Jewish quarter (Me'a She'arim) both men and women must wear something on their head, and women must wear long-sleeved clothing. Anyone wearing shorts or short-sleeved shirts, etc., will be refused entry to many of the Christian sites.

Currency

The unit of currency is the Israeli Shekel (IS) which is made up of 100 Agorot.

There are banknotes for $\frac{1}{2}$, 1, 5, 10 and 50 (new) Shekels.

Exchange rates fluctuate, so it is advisable to consult a bank before departure. For most visitors from abroad, however, the rate is likely to be favourable which makes a holiday in Israel good value for money.

Currency regulations

There are no restrictions on importing Israeli or foreign currency (cash, traveller's cheques, letters of credit, Israel Bonds) but it is advisable to declare how much foreign currency you bring with you. Foreign currency can be exported up to the amount declared on entry but only up to 500 Israeli Shekels may be taken out of the country.

Changing money

Money can be changed at any bank, many of which also have branches in the main hotels. Payment for goods and services can be made in almost any kind of foreign currency.

There is, however, no legal obligation to accept foreign currency. Change is usually given in shekels.

Discounts

All goods and services are subject to value added tax.

There is no VAT on furs bought at one of the official shops (displaying two figures with a bunch of grapes) and paid for in foreign currency and a 25% discount is granted for leather goods but the goods in question are not handed over until departure from the country.

Anyone paying in foreign currency in one of these official shops for goods to a value of more than 50 U.S. dollars gets a discount of at least 5% and the value added tax will also be returned if the receipt is produced on leaving the country.

The following services are not subject to value added tax provided payment is made in foreign currency: flights by Israeli airlines, scheduled tours and charters, including meals consumed en route, hotel meals and accommodation, if the bill is endorsed accordingly, official hiring of a private car and vehicle hire if this includes a driver acting as a guide.

Customs regulations

On entry. – Personal effects and tourist items may be temporarily imported free of duty. This includes 2 cameras and 1 cine-camera (up to 16 mm) with 10 rolls of film each, 1 portable typewriter, 1 tape recorder with 700 m of tape, 1 record player with records, 1 portable radio, a pair of binoculars, tools, musical instruments, fishing and sports equipment, 1 bicycle and camping equipment.

These items must be declared on entry. You may be asked to provide a guarantee for portable television sets or diving equipment. No duty is charged on the following items for private consumption: 250 cigarettes or 250 g tobacco, 2 litres wine, 1 litre spirits, 0·25 litre of perfume, gifts up to a value of equivalent to 125 U.S. dollars. It is forbidden to import drugs, knives with fixed blades and clasp-knives with blades longer than 10 cm (4 in.), as well as fresh meat and fruit.

Cars, trailers and boats may also be imported duty-free, and import permits valid for one year are issued at the border. Foreign visitors' cars remain free of duty for three months.

On departure. – On re-entry into Britain from Israel the duty-free allowances are 200 cigarettes *or* 100 cigarillos *or* 50 cigars *or* 250 g tobacco; 1 litre of alcohol of more than 38·8° proof *or* 2 litres of alcohol of not more than 38·8° proof *or* 2 litres of fortified or sparkling wine *plus* 2 litres of table-wine, 50 g perfume and 0·25 litre toilet water and other articles up to a value of £28.

The duty-free allowances are approximately one-third greater for goods bought in the ordinary shops in EEC countries but not for goods bought in a duty-free shop, on a ship or on an aircraft.

Doctors

See First aid

Electricity

The power supply in Israel is 220 V AC. Since most plugs are three-pin it is advisable to take an adapter for electric razors, hair-dryers, etc. Adapters can also be obtained in Jerusalem.

Embassies

American Embassy
71 Hayarkon Street
Tel Aviv
tel. (03) 25 43 38

British Embassy
192 Hayarkon Street
Tel Aviv
tel. (03) 24 91 71

Canadian Embassy
220 Hayarkon Street
Tel Aviv
tel. (03) 22 81 22

Emergency calls

Ambulance, tel. 101
Fire brigade, tel. 102
Police, tel. 100

First aid

Emergency number

101

Magen David Adom
("Red Star of David")

This number for emergencies contacts Magen David Adom, the
Israeli equivalent of the Red Cross, which is responsible for first
aid posts, ambulances and Israel's blood bank.
Its central first aid post is in the Romema district (tel. 101).
There is another one near the Dung Gate (tel. 28 24 95).

Food and drink

Israel does not have a true cuisine of its own. Its dishes are
either Western European or Arab. Here, though, one can find
everything from Russian borsch to American hamburgers, not
to mention pizza and hot-dogs.

Kosher

Food that is kosher, i.e. pure, has been prepared in accordance
with the Jewish dietary laws based originally on the need for
hygiene. Kosher restaurants do not serve pork, game, some
types of poultry or the flesh of invertebrates, while meat and
dairy products must not be served during the same meal. Five
hours have to elapse after eating meat before one can eat dairy
products.
Although some say that kosher is dull it is worth trying it for
yourself because it does include some very tasty dishes, the
best-known being gefilte fish and chopped chicken liver.

Alcohol

Israel has no laws on drink and driving. The reason for this is the
fact that very little alcohol is drunk in Israel.
Parties and social gatherings normally start with a sip of brandy
from minute glasses but that is the sum total of spirits for the
evening.
On the other hand, there are some very good Israeli wines (red,
white, rosé, sweet and dry).
The local beers may have a very low alcohol content but they
are very palatable.

Hospices

The hospices run by the different Christian communities offer
inexpensive accommodation, usually with full board. It is
advisable to book in advance, particularly during the Christian
holidays. A list of these hospices can be obtained from any
Israel Government Tourist Office (see Information) as well as
from the Israel Pilgrimage Committee, P.O.B. 1018, Jerusalem.

A kosher menu also has a lot to offer ▶

לשוב
נא להכין כר

& HOLIDAYS.
ETS IN ADVANCE

JERUSALEM RESTAURANT
KASHER
PRICE LIST

		שקל
STEAK	with 2 vegetables, soup, pudding, bread	27-
BEEF LIVER	with 2 vegetables, soup, pudding, bread	25-
GRILLED CHICKEN	with 2 vegetables, soup, pudding, bread	25-
SHISHLIK	with 2 vegetables, soup, pudding, bread	25-
POT ROAST	with 2 vegetables, soup, pudding, bread	25-
VIENNA SCHNITZEL	with 2 vegetables, soup, pudding, bread	25-
KABAB	with 2 vegetables, soup, pudding, bread	25-
ROAST BEEF	with 2 vegetables, soup, pudding, bread	25-
BEEF GOULASH	with 2 vegetables, soup, pudding, bread	25-
CHICKEN LIVER	with 2 vegetables, soup, pudding, bread	27-
FRESH CARP	with 2 vegetables, soup, pudding, bread	25-
FISH FILET	with 2 vegetables, soup, pudding, bread	21-
GEFILLTE FISH	with 2 vegetables, soup, pudding, bread	21-
MEAT BALLS	with 2 vegetables, soup, pudding, bread	21-
GOOSE SALAMI	with 2 vegetables, soup, pudding, bread	21-
SAUSAGES	with 2 vegetables, soup, pudding, bread	21-
EGG with MAYONAISE	with 2 vegetables, soup, pudding, bread	19-
VEGETABLE PLATE	with 3 vegetables, soup, pudding, bread	19-
HUMUS OR TEHINA with PITA		6-

V.A.T. INCLUDED

Practical Information

English Hospices	St George's Hostel, Nablus Road and Saladin Street
	St Andrew's Scots Memorial Hospice, near Railway Station
	Christ Church Hospice, Jaffa Gate
	Centre Notre Dame, opposite New Gate

Hospitals

Hospitals that take emergency cases are listed in the daily newspapers. Generally speaking, in the event of illness it is advisable to contact Magen David Adom (tel. 101) which corresponds to the Red Cross and operates first aid posts, an ambulance service and Israel's blood bank. The first aid post of Magen David Adom can be found near the Dung Gate in the S of the old town.

| First aid posts | See First aid |
| Emergency calls | See Emergency calls |

Hotels (selection)

Categories	L=Luxury=officially 5 stars
	I, II, III=categories 1–3=officially 4–2 stars
	(k)=kosher, r.=rooms, SP=swimming pool
	Hotels in category I (4 stars) are of a superior standard

In the west	*Jerusalem Hilton (k). Givat Ram, L, 420 r., tennis
	*Jerusalem Plaza (k), 47 Ha-Melekh George, L, 414 r., SP, sauna
	*King David (k), 23 David Ha-Melekh, L, 258 r., SP, sauna, tennis
	*King Solomon Sheraton (k), 32 David Ha-Melekh, 150 r., sauna
	Ramada Shalom (k), Bayit we-Gan, I, 594 r., SP, sauna
	Moriah (k), 39 Keren Ha-Yessod, I, 301 r.
	Kings (k), 60 Ha-Melekh George, I, 214 r.
	Ariel (k), 31 Derekh Hevron, I, 140 r.
	Holyland (k), 1 Bayit we-Gan, I, 120 r., SP, tennis
	Central (k), 6 Pines Mikhal I, 77 r.
	Torat Bat Sheva (k), 42 Ha-Melekh George, I, 70 r.
	Jerusalem Tadmor (k), 1 Ha-Gay (Bet Ha-Kerem), I, 51 r.
	Sonesta Jerusalem, 2 Wolfson Street, II, 172 r.
	Ram (k), 234 Yafo, II, 156 r.
	Windmill, 3 Mendele Street, II, 133 r.
	Eilon Tower, 34 Ben Yehuda Street, II, 120 r.
	Jerusalem Tower (k), 23 Hillel, II, 120 r.
	Y.M.C.A., 26 David Ha-Melekh, II, 68 r., SP, tennis
	The Menora, 24 David Ha-Melekh, II, 64 r.
	Neve Shoshana (k), 5 Bet Ha-Kerem, II, 27 r.
	Rama Gidron (k), 15 En Zurim (Talpiyyot), II, 16 r.
	Palatin (k), 4 Agrippas, III, 28 r.
	Ron (k), 42A Yafo, III, 22 r.
	Har Aviv (k), 16A Bet Ha-Kerem, III, 14 r.

| In the East | *Diplomat (k), 6 Ezyon (Talpiyyot), L, 400 r., SP |
| | *Intercontinental, Mount of Olives, L, 200 r., tennis |

Ariel Hotel

Model of Herod I's Jerusalem in the garden of the Holyland Hotel

*St George, Salah ed-Din, L, 150 r., SP
*Mount Scopus, Sheikh Jarrah, L, 65 r.
Ambassador, Sheikh Jarrah, I, 118 r.
National Palace, 4 Az Zahra, I, 108 r.
Ritz, 8 Ibn Khaldun, I, 103 r.
American Colony, Derekh Shekhem, I, 102 r.
Panorama, Mount of Olives (Gethsemane), I, 74 r.
Capitol, Salah ed-Din, I, 54 r.
Holyland East, 6 Harun el-Rashid, II, 105 r.
Pilgrim's Palace, near Herod's Gate, II, 95 r.
Palace, adjacent to Shemu'el Ben Adaya, II, 68 r.
Gloria, near the Jaffa Gate, II, 64 r.
Y.M.C.A., Aelia Capitolina, 29 Nablus Road, II, 57 r., tennis
Strand, Ibn Jubeir, II, 55 r.
Shepherd, Mount Scopus, II, 52 r.
Commodore, Mount of Olives, II, 45 r.
Y.W.C.A., Wadi el-Joz, II, 30 r.
Jordan House, Nur el-Din, II, 25 r.
New Metropole, 8 Salah ed-Din, II, 25 r.
Christmas, Salah ed-Din, II, 24 r.
Mount of Olives, Shemu'el Ben Adaya, III, 63 r.
Vienna East, Sheikh Jarrah, III, 39 r.
Rivoli, 3 Salah ed-Din, III, 31 r.
Lawrence, 18 Salah ed-Din, III, 30 r.
Metropole, 6 Salah ed-Din, III, 30 r.
Az Zahra, 13 Az Zahra, III, 24 r.
Astoria, Shemu'el Ben Adaya, III, 23 r.
City, Sheikh Jarrah, III, 22 r.
New Orient House (k), American Colony, III, 22 r.
Park Lane, Derekh Shekhem, III, 20 r.

Information

Israel Government Tourist Office
18 Great Marlborough Street
London W1V 1AF
tel. (01) 434 3651

Israel Government Tourist Office
350 Fifth Avenue
New York
New York 10118
tel. (212) 560 0650

5 South Wabash Avenue
Chicago, Illinois 60603
tel. (312) 782 4306

6380 Wilshire Boulevard
Los Angeles
California 90048
tel. (213) 658 7462

4151 Southwest Freeway
Houston
Texas 77027
tel. (713) 850 9341

Israel Government Tourist Office
102 Bloor Street West
Toronto
Ontario M5S 1M(8)
tel. (416) 964 3784

Israel Government Tourist Office   In Jerusalem
24 Ha-Melekh George, tel. 24 12 81
Open: Sun.–Thurs. 8 a.m.–6 p.m., Fri. and the day before public
holidays 8 a.m.–3 p.m.

Israel Government Tourist Office
Jaffa Gate, tel. 28 22 95/6
Open: Sun.–Thurs. 8 a.m.–6 p.m., Fri. and the day before public
holidays 8 a.m.–3 p.m., Sat. and public holidays 10 a.m.–2 p.m.

Municipal Tourist Information Office
34 Yafo Road, tel. 22 88 44
Open: Sun.–Thurs. 8 a.m.–6 p.m., Fri. and the day before public
holidays 8 a.m.–2 p.m.

Members of the voluntary tourist service are available from   Voluntary tourist service
Sun.–Thurs. between 5 and 7.30 p.m. (not on public holidays)
in the following hotels: King David, Hilton, Moriah, Plaza,
Kings, Holyland, Ramada Shalom, Diplomat (see Hotels entry
for addresses).

Information from the Jerusalem Office in Yafo Road, tel.
28 81 40.

Language

The official languages are Modern Hebrew (Ivrit, the revised
language of the Old Testament) and Arabic.
Since Israel is basically a State composed of immigrants it is
possible to communicate in almost all the European languages,
particularly English, French and German. English is used for
business.

Libraries and archives

Gulbenkian Tourian Library
Armenian Monastery (Old Town), Mon.–Fri. 3.30–6 p.m.

Jerusalem City Library
Branch libraries in every district of the city

Jewish National and University Library
See A–Z, Hebrew University

W. F. Albright Institute of Archaeological Research
Salah ed-Din, tel. 28 21 31

165

Library of the Dominican monastery of St Stephen
Derekh Shekhem, tel. 28 22 13

Library of the École Biblique et Archéologique
See A–Z, St Stephen

Library of El Aqsa Mosque
See A–Z, Haram esh-Sharif
Islamic Museum

Library of the Greek-Orthodox Patriarchate
Near Jaffa Gate, Mon.–Sat. 9 a.m.–12.30 p.m.

Library of the Hebrew University, History Institute
See A–Z, Hebrew University

Library of the Israel Museum
See A–Z, Israel Museum

Library of the Protestant-Lutheran Community
Bet Ha Bad, near the Church of the Redeemer

Library of the Rav-Kook Institute
Ha-Rav Maimon, tel. 52 62 31

Library of the Rockefeller Museum
See A–Z, Rockefeller Museum

Library of the Yad Vashem Monument
See A–Z, Yad Vashem

Library of the Yeshurun Central Synagogue
Ha-Melekh George
Open: Sun.–Thurs. 4–9 p.m.

Library of the Zionist Central Authorities
See A–Z, Zionist Central Authorities

Papal Bible Institute
Paul Emile Botta Street
Open: Mon.–Sat. 9 a.m.–noon

Salman Shocken Library
6 Rechov Balfour

Museums

Agricultural Museum
13 Heleni Ha-Malka
Open: Summer: Sun.–Fri. 8 a.m.–1 p.m.; Winter: Sun.–Thurs.
8 a.m.–2 p.m., Fri. 8 a.m.–1 p.m.
Agricultural implements including some pre-Christian ones.

Armenian Art and History Museum
See A–Z, Armenian Quarter

Biblical Zoo
Kiryat Zanz
Open: 8 a.m. (in winter 8.30 a.m.) until sunset; guided tours (in English): Wed. and Sun. 4 p.m. (July–Sept.), 2 p.m. (Oct.–June).
Tickets for Saturday must be bought in advance (Sinbad Tourist Agency in the Salah-ed Din, the Express Shop next to the Scopus Hotel, etc.).
The Biblical Zoo houses almost all the animals mentioned in the Bible. The setting is that of a country park rather than that of a typical zoo.

David Palombo Museum
Mount Zion
Open: Sun.–Thurs. 10.30 a.m.–4.30 p.m., Fri. 9.30 a.m.–1 p.m.

Giv'at Tahomshet
Sederot Levi Eshkol, Ramot Eshkol
Open: daily 9 a.m.–1 p.m.
Museum commemorating Israeli soldiers who fell in the Six Day War. The museum contains models and maps and is set in a park with trenches and bunkers.

Hakhal Shlomo
See A–Z, Chief Rabbinate

Hall of Heroes
Migrash ha Russim
Open: Sun.–Thurs. 10 a.m.–4 p.m., Fri. and the day before public holidays 10 a.m.–1 p.m. Closed Sat. and public holidays.
The work of the underground movement during the British mandate and during the fight for independence is shown in the former Jerusalem state prison which is now a museum.

Herbert Clark Collection
Y.M.C.A. House
Open: daily, except Sun. and Wed., 10 a.m.–1 p.m.
Near East antiquities from pre-historic times until the Arabian period.

Herzl Museum
See A–Z, Mount Herzl

Islamic Museum
See A–Z, Haram esh-Sharif

Israel Museum
See A–Z, Israel Museum

Jerusalem Museum
See A–Z, Citadel

L. A. Mayer Memorial Institute for Islamic Art
2 Ha-Palmah
Open: Sun., Mon., Tues., Thurs. 10 a.m.–12.30 p.m., 3.30–6 p.m., Wed. 3.30–9 p.m., Sat. 10.30 a.m.–1 p.m.
Tickets for Saturday must be obtained from the museum in advance.
Islamic art from different periods and countries (ceramics, carpets, textiles, miniatures), graphics; excellent collection of European and Ottoman clocks and musical instruments; archives, library.

Montefiore Windmill
Mishkenot Sha-ananim
Open: Sun.–Thurs. 3–6 p.m., Sat. and public holidays 10 a.m.–
2 p.m., 4–7 p.m. Closed Fri.
The exhibits chart the history of the Yemin Moshe quarter
which was the first district to be settled outside the old town
walls.

Museum of Italian-Jewish Art
27 Hillel Street
Open: Sun. 10 a.m.–1 p.m., Wed. 4–7 p.m.

Museum of Musical Instruments
7 Rehov Smolenskin
Open: Sun.–Fri. 10 a.m.–1 p.m.

Natural History Museum
6 Rehov Mohilever
Open: Sun.–Thurs. 9 a.m.–1 p.m., Mon. and Wed. also 4–6 p.m.,
Sat. 10.30 a.m.–1 p.m. Closed Fri.
Birds, mammals, special anatomy departments, dioramas and
working models.

Old Yishuv Court Museum
6 Rehov Or Hahayyim, Old Town, Jewish quarter
Open: Sun.–Thurs. 9 a.m.–4 p.m.
A restored 19th c. house is the setting for displays of utensils,
etc., and authentic interiors that show how the Jewish
inhabitants of the Old Town lived in the period from the 19th c.
up to 1948. Also on view is a synagogue for Ashkenazi Jews
(from Central and Eastern Europe) and Sephardi Jews (from
Spain and Portugal).

Papal Bible Museum
Paul Emile Botta
Open: Mon.–Thurs. 9 a.m.–noon. Closed on Sun. and Roman
Catholic Holidays.
Archaeological museum and comprehensive library.

Quality Warehouse
12 Hebron Str.
Open: Sun.–Thurs. 10 a.m.–7 p.m., Fri. 10 a.m.–1 p.m.
Craft centre including studios and workshops.

Rockefeller Museum
See A–Z, Rockefeller Museum

Schocken Institute of Jewish Research
6 Balfour
Open: Sun.–Thurs. 9 a.m.–1 p.m.
Jewish illuminated manuscripts from the 13th c. onwards,
autography and about 50 incunabula.

Sir Isaac and Lady Wolfson Museum
Ha-Melekh George (in the Chief Rabbinate building)
Open: Sun.–Thurs. 9 a.m.–1 p.m., Fri. 9 a.m.–noon.
Jewish exhibits of various periods.

Tax Museum
32 Rehov Agron
Open: Mon., Wed., Fri. 10 a.m.–2 p.m.

Yad Vashem
See A–Z, Yad Vashem

Music

Performances by the Israeli Philharmonic Orchestra and other
ensembles are given at the following venues:

Concerts, chamber music

Artists' House
12 Rehov Shemu'el Hanagid

Bet ha-'Am
Bezalel

Binyene ha-'Umma
Giv'at Ram

International Cultural Centre for Youth (I.C.C.Y.)
12A Emeq Refa'im

Israel Museum
See A–Z, Israel Museum: Library

Khan Centre
Opposite the station

Jerusalem Theatre
Chopin Street
Mitchell Auditorium
Strauss Street (in the Histadruth House)

Rubin Music Academy
7 Rehov Smolenskin

Wise Auditorium
On the Hebrew University campus, Giv'at Ram

The Israeli spring festival of music, theatre and dance (see
Calendar of events) is internationally famous.
Further details can be obtained from the ticket agencies and
information offices (see Information).

Spring festival

Folk dance and dance groups are very popular in Israel. The
most famous of these groups are Inbal, the Bat Sheva Dance
Company and the Bat Dor Dance Company. Programmes for
the current week can be obtained at hotels or from the
information offices (see Information).

Folk dance

169

Practical Information

Every Monday and Wednesday at 9 p.m. in the Y.M.C.A. auditorium, 26 David Ha-Melekh, there is an evening of Jewish and Arab folklore.

Ballet

When glancing through the weekly programme you should keep an eye out for the Israel Classical Ballet (classical ballet only), the Bat Dor Dance Company and the Bat Sheva Dance Company. The last two have specialised in modern ballet.

Night life

One should not expect to find a Soho or a Place Pigalle in the holy city of Jerusalem.

Its "night life" is more likely to take the form of a civilised drink in the bar of one of the big hotels or simply a meal in a restaurant during an evening of folk song and dance. Unlike other big cities there are no sex-shows with their neon signs.

Night clubs

Jerusalem does have plenty of night clubs but the floor-shows are rather refined and few of them offer more informal entertainment. One has to pay for at least one drink.

Discotheques

In the discos you can dance to pop, jazz and sometimes even rock music as well.

Opening times (Sabbath: Fri. 3.59 p.m.–Sat. 5.14 p.m.)

Banks

Sun., Mon., Tues., Thurs. 8.30 a.m.–12.30 p.m., 4–5 or 5.30 p.m. Wed. 8.30 a.m.–12.30 p.m., Fri. 8.30 a.m.–noon. Some banks have branches in the larger hotels which also provide a service outside the usual opening times.

Chemists

Sun.–Thurs. 8.30 a.m.–1 p.m., 4–7 p.m., Fri. 9.30 a.m.–2 p.m. For chemists that are open at night (see Chemists) see the daily newspapers.

Museums

Museum opening times are given either in the A–Z under the name of the museum or under the "Museums" heading in the practical information.

Post offices

As a general rule Sun.–Thurs. 8 a.m.–6 p.m., Fri. 8 a.m.–2 p.m.

Public transport

Apart from a few bus lines operated by Arabs there are no trains or buses running in Israel from late on Friday afternoon until Saturday evening.

Shops

Shops are generally open from 8.30 a.m. to 1 p.m., and 4 to 7 p.m. The smaller foodshops open early in the morning. Jewish shops are open on Fridays from 8.30 a.m. to 2 p.m. and then shut until Sunday morning. Christian shops are shut on Sundays and Moslem shops shut on Fridays.

Passport

See Travel documents

Petrol stations

In West Jerusalem nearly all the petrol stations are closed from Friday evening until Saturday evening. They are open, however, in East Jerusalem.

Post offices

Because of mounting inflation postal rates cannot be given. It is advisable to send one's post by airmail in any case. Letters to Europe can be expected to take about 10 days.

Stamps can be obtained from stationers, shops, souvenir shops, bookshops and the big hotels as well as from post offices.

Stamps

The sign for a post office is a leaping stag in white on a blue background.

Post offices

Head post office:
Yafo Road, Kikkar Bar Kokhva

Sub post offices:
Keren Kayemet (opposite the Jewish Agency)
Shammay Street
Suleiman corner Salah ed-Din (near Herod's Gate)
Citadel (near the Jaffa Gate)

Pillar boxes are painted red and carry the sign of the stag.

Pillar boxes

See Opening hours

Opening times

See Telephone

Telephoning

See Telegrams

Telegrams

Programme of events

A brochure obtainable from hotels and tourist information offices (see Information) gives details of the current week's events.

Public holidays

It is not easy to sort out the system of public holidays in Israel because the country has Jewish, Christian and Moslem public holidays, plus the fact that one has to distinguish public holidays for the Christian churches of the West (Roman Catholic and Protestant) and the Christian churches of the East (Greek Orthodox and Armenian).

It is not possible to give the exact dates because many of the Christian holidays are movable feasts and Jewish and Moslem holidays are determined by the moon which means that they fall on a different day in the Gregorian calendar every year.

See Calendar of events for a brief explanation of the public holidays.

Jewish

Jewish shops and undertakings (public transport, etc.) shut on Friday afternoons and the Sabbath (Saturday). For the Jews the day starts in the evening so that a Jewish day of rest begins at sunset the day before and ends at sunset on the day of rest itself. This can be traced back to 1:5 in the Book of Genesis: "and the evening and the morning were the first day".

Holiday	Hebrew Date	Gregorian Date
Rosh Hashana (New Year)	1–2 Tishri	Sept./Oct.
Yom Kippur (Day of Atonement)	10 Tishri	Sept./Oct.
Sukkoth (Tabernacles)	15–21 Tishri	Sept./Oct.
Simhath Torah (Rejoicing over the Torah)	22nd Tishri	Sept./Oct.
Hanukkah[1] (Festival of Lights)	25 Kislev	Nov./Dec.
Tu B'Shevat (New Year of the Trees)	15 Shevat	Jan./Feb.
Purim (Festival of Queen Esther)	14 Adar	Feb./March
Pesach (Passover)	15–21 Nissan	March/Apr.
Independence Day	5 Iyar	Apr./May
Lag Ba Omer[1] (33rd day of the Omer)	18 Iyar	Apr./May
Jerusalem Day (Liberation of the city)	28 Iyar	May/June
Shavuot (Feast of Weeks)	6 Sivan	May/June
Tish B'av[1]	9 Av	July/Aug.

[1]As a general rule shops remain open and public transport operates on these public holidays.

Christian

All Christian shops and businesses close on Sundays. The major holidays are: New Year (Western churches: 1 January; Eastern churches: 14 January), Epiphany, Palm Sunday, Good Friday, Easter, Ascension Day, Whitsun and Christmas (Western churches: 24/25 December; Eastern churches: 7 January).

Moslem shops and businesses close on Fridays. The major holidays are:

Id el-Adha (Sacrificial celebrations)	Dec./Jan.
New Year	Jan./Feb.
Mohammed's birthday	April
1st day of Ramadan, the month of fasting	Oct.
Id el-Fitr (last 3 days of Ramadan)	Oct./Nov.

Public transport

The principal means of passenger transport is by bus and one is never far from a bus stop anywhere in Jerusalem. The main points for changing buses are at the Jaffa Gate and the Damascus Gate. (See also Stations.)

Bus

The Sherut taxis normally only operate between the larger cities (see Taxis) but there are also a few stops inside Jerusalem. These seven-seater shared taxis can also be hailed in the street.

Sherut taxi

Radio/television

"Kol Israel" (the voice of Israel) broadcasts foreign language news on its Fourth Programme channel at the following times:
In English 7 a.m., 1 p.m., 5 p.m., 8 p.m.
In French 7.15 a.m., 2.30 p.m., 6.05 p.m., 8.15 p.m.

Radio

Almost all television programmes are in Modern Hebrew and Arabic. Occasionally international films in their original language are shown with subtitles. Programmes are published in the daily newspapers.

Television

Restaurants

Several addresses in addition to those in hotels:

Agron Press Club, 37 Hillel Street, 1st floor (kosher, French)
Alla Gondola, 14 Ha-Melekh George (Italian)
Au Sahara, 17 Rehov Yafo (kosher, Moroccan)
Chez Simon, 15 Shammay (French)
Chung Ching, 122 Herzl Boulevard (kosher, Chinese)
El Marrakesh, 4 David Ha-Melekh (kosher, Continental)
Fink's, 13 Ha-Melekh George (European)
Goulash Inn, En Keran (Hungarian)
Hameshek, 14 Shlomzion Hamalka Street (kosher, vegetarian)
Leah, 15 Keren Hayesod (Hungarian)
Mandy Tatchi, 3 Rehov Hyrkanos (Chinese)
Mishkenot Sha'ananaim, Yemin Moshe Street (kosher, French)
Petra, 11 Harun el-Rashid (oriental)
Sea Dolphin, Harun el-Rashid (fish restaurant)
Stark, 21 Ha-Melekh George (kosher, European)
The Citadel, 14 Hamezuda, Hativat
Yerushalaim (good views, cafeteria)

Shipping companies

	For sailings to and from Israel
Great Britain	Associated Oceanic Agencies 109–110 Jermyn Street London SW1Y 6ES, tel. 01–930 9534/7449

Sol Maritime
c/o Cyprus Travel London Ltd
42 Hampstead Road
London NW1, tel. 01–387 7854

Zenon Travel & Tours
15 Kentish Town Road
London NW1, tel. 01–267 0269/2657

Lykes Lines
Lykes Bros. Steamship Co. Inc.
Lykes Center, 300 Poydras Street
New Orleans, Louisiana 70130, tel. (504) 523 6611

Prudential Lines Inc.
Room 3701, One World Trade Center
New York 10048, tel. 524 8212/8217

U.S.A.   World Dynamics Travel
New York, tel. 212 697 4224

Sightseeing

On foot

The Government Tourist Office (see Information) organises guided tours (generally in English) of various kinds: circuit on foot on the old town walls, daily except Saturday and public holidays, 9 a.m.–4.30 p.m., from Zion Gate.

"Jerusalem through the Centuries" (from the Citadel Court-yard; about 3 hours, in English): Sun. at 9.30 a.m. and 2 p.m., Mon. at 11 a.m. and 2 p.m., Tues. at 9.30 a.m., Wed. at 11 a.m., Thurs. and Fri. at 9.30 a.m.

Also: Mon. at 9.30 a.m. Jewish Quarter (from car park in the Jewish Quarter); Wed. at 2.30 p.m., excavations at the Western Wall (from Dung Gate); Thurs. at 11 a.m. various places of interest (duration 2 hours); Sat. at 9 a.m. interesting places in the surroundings of the city (from King Solomon Sheraton Hotel, 32 King David Street); Sat. at 10 a.m. various places of interest in the city (from Tourist Information, 34 Jaffa Road). Visitors should confirm details of each event.

By coach

Seats on coach tours must be booked in advance. Tours are organised by the following operators:

Egged Tours
44a Yafo (Kikkar Ziyyon), tel. 22 41 98
224 Yafo (by the central bus station), tel. 561 11

Eshkolot Tours
36 Keren Ha-Yessod, tel. 63 55 55, 66 55 55

Neot Hakikar
36 Keren Ha-Yessod, tel. 63 64 94, 69 93 85

United Tours
King David Hotel extension, tel. 22 21 87

Yehuda Tours
23 Hillel, tel. 22 77 40

These companies also operate excursions inland lasting between half a day and three days either by partially air-conditioned coach or on a "fly and ride" basis. These are accompanied by multilingual official tour guides.

It is possible to hire a seven-seater minibus with a licensed guide who also acts as the driver. Details are available from the tourist information offices (see Information).

By Minibus

Sport

There is no professional sport in Israel. Most international meetings are held in Tel Aviv but Jerusalem does have centres catering for sport of all kinds.
The most popular form of sport is football followed by basketball, watersports and tennis.

Y.M.C.A.
See A–Z, Y.M.C.A.

Sports centres

Jerusalem Sports Club
Ha-Zefira, tel. 63 21 25
Buses: 4, 18

Nearly all hotels have their own tennis courts. Other tennis venues include:

Tennis

A.A.C.I. (Moadon ha'Oleh)
9 Alkalay, tel. 63 37 18
Bus: 15
Courts must be booked in advance

A.S.A.
Hebrew University Givat Ram, tel. 66 78 94

See Swimming pools

Swimming

Stations

Central Bus Station
Yafo Road (Romema district), tel. 55 17 11
Buses: 6, 8, 9, 10, 15, 18, 20, 25, 27

Bus

Buses are Israel's main means of passenger transport, both in town and, at a very reasonable price, cross-country. Regular bus services leave from the central bus station in Romema for destinations all over the country.
Except for the bus lines operated by Arabs there are no buses on the Sabbath (Saturday) or on Jewish public holidays and the evening before.

Practical Information

Railway
Railway Station
Kikkar Remez, tel. 71 77 64
Buses: 4, 6, 7, 8, 10, 14

Israel does not have a very extensive rail network but there are trains between the country's major cities (Haifa, Tel Aviv). There is a buffet car on every passenger train and it costs less to travel by train than by bus. Trains do not run on the Sabbath (Saturday), on Friday evenings or on Jewish public holidays and the evening before.

Swimming pools

The season for swimming outdoors lasts from the end of May until the end of September. During the season swimming pools are open from 8 a.m. until 5 p.m. A list of all swimming pools is obtainable from the tourist information offices (see Information). All the big hotels also have their own swimming pools. In winter it is also possible to go swimming in the Dead Sea.

Beit Taylor
Qiryat Hayovel, tel. 41 43 62
Bus: 18

Diplomat Hotel
Talpiot, tel. 71 08 31
Bus: 8

Holyland
Bayit we-Gan, tel. 66 11 01
Bus: 6/1

Jerusalem Swimming Pool
Rechov Emek Refaim, tel. 63 20 92
Buses: 4, 18

King David Hotel
David Ha-Melekh, tel. 22 11 11
Buses: 6, 7, 15, 18

President Hotel
Rechov Achad Ha'am, tel. 63 12 73
Buses: 4, 15

In the Judean Hills
Kibbutz Ma'ala ha'Hamisha
Kibbutz Ramat Rachel
Moshav Bet Sait
Moshav Shoresh

Taxis

Within Jerusalem
Jerusalem has a great many taxi firms. Every taxi has to have a meter and may only charge at the official rate. Drivers must show passengers the farescale if requested. Taxi-rides at night are subject to an extra 25%.

Trips between the larger cities in the seven-seater Sherut taxis are slightly more expensive but considerably more comfortable than in the cross-country buses. There is an official farescale and a surcharge is payable at night.

There are no Sherut taxis on Saturdays and Jewish holidays apart from those not operated by Jews and for which a surcharge is payable.
Taxis can be booked by telephone from the following firms:

Aviv
4 Dorot Rishonim, tel. 22 73 66
to Tel Aviv and Haifa

Joel Daroma
2 Lunz, tel. 22 69 85
to Beer Sheva and Eilat

Kesher
6 Lunz, tel. 22 23 50
to Tel Aviv

Merkas Habira
3 Lunz, tel. 22 45 45
to Tel Aviv

Nesher
21 Ha-Melekh George, tel, 22 72 27
to Ben Gurion International Airport

Telephone

From the United States: 011 972
From the United Kingdom: 010 972
From Canada: 011 972

From Israel to the United States: 00 1
From Israel to the United Kingdom: 00 44
From Israel to Canada: 00 1

When dialling from Israel the zero prefixed to the local dialling code should be omitted.

Local calls can be made from coin-operated telephones. There are different ways of using these so be careful to follow the instructions. The requisite coins (asimonim) can be obtained from post offices (see Post offices) and kiosks.

Local calls

Telephone calls can also be made in cafés, restaurants, hotels and chemists but in most cases they will cost twice as much.

Although there is direct dialling for most of Israel, it is seldom possible to use the public telephones for international calls (apart from the fact that most of the time spent on a call to Europe would be taken up with feeding in the money). The post office is still the best place to make an international call. Most post office international calls can be dialled direct and you can get through almost immediately.

International calls

Telegrams

Telegrams can be sent from any post office (see Post offices) but at night and on Saturdays this can only be done at the Head Post Office.

Tourist information

See Information

Travel documents

For a stay of less than three months nationals of the United Kingdom and other Western countries only require a full passport (which means that holidays on British Visitors Passports do not qualify). This full passport must be valid for at least nine more months. Children under 16 must either have their own full passport or be entered on the passport of one of their parents. Americans and Canadians require a visitor's visa, which is issued free of charge at the port of entry.

It is also worth noting that Arab countries, except Egypt, will refuse entry to anyone with an Israeli stamp or visa (even if it is out of date). Visitors who require a visa should ask the immigration officials to put it on their AL-17 entering form and not in their passport.

Transit visa

Should you wish to stay in Israel on your way to other destinations, you can obtain a transit visa, valid for five days, from any Israel embassy or consulate. It can be extended for a further ten days after your arrival in Israel.

If you visit Israel on a cruise ship, you will be given a Landing-for-the-day Card, which permits you to remain in the country as long as your ship is in port, and you need not apply for a visitor's visa.

Collective visa

Collective visas are issued by Israel embassies or consulates to groups of not less than five and not more than 50 persons.

Extension of stay

An extension of stay may be obtained at any one of the district offices of the Ministry of the Interior. This generally requires the stamping of your passport.

Vaccination regulations

Since the elimination of smallpox (World Health Congress resolution WHA 34, 13, 1981) vaccination is no longer necessary for entry into Israel.

Travel to Israel

Most European and North American visitors to Israel travel by air. There are direct flights between the main International airports and Tel Aviv (Ben Gurion international airport at Lod).

The flight to Israel takes 4½ hours from London, 10½ hours from New York and 10 hours from Montreal.

It is a good idea to compare prices and consider whether it is cheaper to take a charter flight rather than a scheduled flight even if it means having to see Jerusalem as part of a group. There are special rates, which can entail considerable reductions, for young people, students and pensioners

It is worth enquiring about special packages, including cheap flight for pilgrims, students, those interested in working in a kibbutz or visiting the archaeological sites.

There are also special arrangements for cyclists in Israel. Details are obtainable from:

The Jerusalem Cyclists' Club
P.O. Box 7281
tel. 24 82 38, 41 25 22

Details can also be obtained from the Israel Government Tourist Office (see Information).

A number of shipping lines operate regular car ferry services, etc., to Haifa from Italian and Greek ports. Passage should be booked at least a month in advance.

For addresses see Shipping companies.

Adriatica:
Venice–Piraeus–Limassol–Haifa.

Hellenic Mediterranean Line:
Venice/Ancona–Piraeus–Rhodes–Limassol–Haifa.

Sol Lines:
Venice–Piraeus–Heraklion–Limassol–Haifa.

Stability Line:
Piraeus–Heraklion–Limassol–Haifa.

As with air travel, it is a good idea to compare prices. The companies' agents (see Shipping companies) will provide information about any special arrangements such as stopping off en route, etc.

Very few European visitors travel by road to Israel. The principal crossing from Egypt is at Nizzane, about 43 miles/70 km SW of Beersheba; from Jordan entry is over the Allenby Bridge, 6 miles/10 km E of Jericho.
Frontier formalities, see Travel documents and Customs regulations.

Charter flights

Special packages

By ship

Shipping routes

By road

When to go

To judge from the floods of visitors that stream into the Holy Places in the summer months one would think that this must be the best time to go.

179

It is very hot, often with temperatures well into the 90s; the air in Jerusalem is relatively dry but the countryside around is sun-scorched and like a desert now that everything that flowered in the short-lived spring has withered and died.

Although spring and autumn are both very brief this can be a pleasant time to travel. The spring is also the only time of year when one can enjoy the almond blossom and the landscape around Jerusalem is one of lush vegetation rather than desert. There are also fewer sightseers to contend with (see also Climate).

Youth hostels

The youth hostels are run by the Israel Youth Hostel Association which is affiliated to the International Youth Hostel Association. There is no upper age limit. Youth hostels have communal dormitories and kitchen facilites. Most of them also serve meals.

Accommodation is also available for family parties in some youth hostels.

Personal bookings should be made with the particular youth hostel in question. Group bookings are taken by the national office of the I.Y.H.A., 3 Rechov Dorot Rishonim, tel. 22 20 73.

In and around Jerusalem

Bar Giora Youth Hostel
Bar Giora, tel. 91 10 73

Bernstein Youth Hostel
2 Keren Ha-Yessod, tel. 22 82 86
Buses: 4, 7, 9, 15, 22

En Kerem
En Kerem, tel. 41 62 82

Ha'Esrachi Youth Hostel
In the Judean Hills, tel. 53 97 70
Bus: From the central bus station in Yafo Road

Ivy Yehuda Youth Hostel
In the Jerusalem Forest, tel. 41 60 60
Only for groups that have booked in advance

Kefar Ezyon
Halfway between Bethlehem and Hebron, tel. 74 15 33
Bus: From the central bus station in Yafo Road
Closed on the Sabbath and Jewish holidays

Louise Waterman Wise Youth Hostel
Bayit we-Gan, tel. 42 33 66
Buses: 6/1, 12, 18, 20, 24

Moreshet Ha-Yahadut
In the Jewish quarter of the Old Town, tel. 28 86 11

Ramat Rachel Kibbutz
tel. 71 03 23
Bus: 8

Ramot Shapira
Bet Me'ir, tel. 91 38 91
Bus: From the central bus station in Yafo Road

Useful telephone Numbers at a Glance

Emergency calls

Ambulance (Magen David Adom)	101
Chemist (Magen David Adom)	101
Dentist	52 31 33/4
Fire brigade	102
First aid (Magen David Adom)	101
Police	100

Tourist information

Israel Government Tourist Office	24 12 81/2
	28 22 95/6
Municipal Tourist Information Office	22 88 44
Tourist services (guided tours)	28 81 40
Information about rail services	71 77 64
Information about bus services	52 11 21

Airlines

Air France	22 26 55
Alitalia	22 86 53
British Airways	23 36 02
El Al	23 33 33
KLM	23 28 81
Olympic Airways	23 45 38
Sabena	23 49 71
SAS	28 32 35
Swissair	23 31 92
TWA	24 11 35/6
I.S.S.T.A. (student flights)	23 14 18
International flight information	(03) 29 55 55

Embassies

Great Britain, Tel Aviv	(03) 24 91 71
United States, Tel Aviv	(03) 25 43 38
Canada, Tel Aviv	(03) 22 81 22

Telegrams 171

Telephone service

Enquiries, national	14
Enquiries, international	195
Recorded information – events	24 11 97

7/2/95

ADDITIONAL SITES

_____

John F. Kennedy Memorial

Notes

Notes

Notes

Notes

Notes

Baedeker's Travel Guides

What's there to do and see in foreign countries? Travelers who rely on Baedeker, one of the oldest names in travel literature, will miss nothing. Baedeker's bright red, internationally recognized covers open up to reveal fascinating A-Z directories of cities, towns, and regions, complete with their sights, museums, monuments, cathedrals, castles, gardens and ancestral homes—an approach that gives the traveler a quick and easy way to plan a vacation itinerary.

And Baedekers are filled with over 200 full colour photos and detailed maps, including a full-size, fold-out roadmap for easy vacation driving. Baedeker—the premier name in travel for over 150 years.

Please send me the books checked below:

☐ **Austria**....................\$16.95
0–13–056127–4

☐ **Caribbean**...................\$16.95
0–13–056143–6

☐ **Costa Brava**...............\$11.95
0–13–055880–X

☐ **Denmark**....................\$16.95
0–13–058124–0

☐ **Egypt**.......................\$16.95
0–13–056358–7

☐ **France**......................\$16.95
0–13–055814–1

☐ **Germany**....................\$16.95
0–13–055830–3

☐ **Great Britain**.............\$16.95
0–13–055855–9

☐ **Greece**......................\$16.95
0–13–056002–2

☐ **Greek Islands**.............\$11.95
0–13–058132–1

☐ **Ireland**.....................\$16.95
0–13–058140–2

☐ **Israel**.......................\$16.95
0–13–056176–2

☐ **Italy**........................\$16.95
0–13–055897–4

☐ **Japan**.......................\$16.95
0–13–056382–X

☐ **Loire**.......................\$11.95
0–13–056375–7

☐ **Mediterranean Islands**.......\$16.95
0–13–056862–7

☐ **Mexico**.....................\$16.95
0–13–056069–3

☐ **Netherlands, Belgium and Luxembourg**.........\$16.95
0–13–056028–6

☐ **Portugal**...................\$16.95
0–13–056135–5

☐ **Provence/Côte d'Azur**.........\$11.95
0–13–056938–0

☐ **Rail Guide to Europe**.........\$16.95
0–13–055971–7

☐ **Rhine**......................\$11.95
0–13–056466–4

☐ **Scandinavia**...............\$16.95
0–13–056085–5

☐ **Spain**......................\$16.95
0–13–055913–X

☐ **Switzerland**...............\$16.95
0–13–056044–8

☐ **Turkish Coast**.............\$11.95
0–13–058173–9

☐ **Tuscany**...................\$11.95
0–13–056482–6

☐ **Yugoslavia**................\$16.95
0–13–056184–3

Please turn the page for an order form and a list of additional Baedeker Guides.

A series of city guides filled with color photographs and detailed maps and floor plans from one of the oldest names in travel publishing:

Please send me the books checked below:

☐ **Amsterdam**.......................$11.95
0–13–057969–6

☐ **Athens**..............................$11.95
0–13–057977–7

☐ **Bangkok**...........................$11.95
0–13–057985–8

☐ **Berlin**...............................$11.95
0–13–367996–9

☐ **Brussels**...........................$11.95
0–13–368788–0

☐ **Budapest**..........................$11.95
0–13–058199–2

☐ **Cologne**............................$11.95
0–13–058181–X

☐ **Copenhagen**.....................$11.95
0–13–057993–9

☐ **Florence**...........................$11.95
0–13–369505–0

☐ **Frankfurt**..........................$11.95
0–13–369570–0

☐ **Hamburg**..........................$11.95
0–13–369687–1

☐ **Hong Kong**.......................$11.95
0–13–058009–0

☐ **Istanbul**............................$11.95
0–13–058207–7

☐ **Jerusalem**.........................$11.95
0–13–058017–1

☐ **London**.............................$11.95
0–13–058025–2

☐ **Madrid**..............................$11.95
0–13–058033–3

☐ **Moscow**............................$11.95
0–13–058041–4

☐ **Munich**.............................$11.95
0–13–370370–3

☐ **New York**..........................$11.95
0–13–058058–9

☐ **Paris**................................$11.95
0–13–058066–X

☐ **Prague**..............................$11.95
0–13–058215–8

☐ **Rome**................................$11.95
0–13058074–0

☐ **San Francisco**...................$11.95
0–13–058082–1

☐ **Singapore**.........................$11.95
0–13–058090–2

☐ **Stuttgart**...........................$11.95
0–13–058223–9

☐ **Tokyo**...............................$11.95
0–13–058108–9

☐ **Venice**..............................$11.95
0–13–058116–X

☐ **Vienna**..............................$11.95
0–13–371303–2

PRENTICE HALL PRESS
Order Department—Travel Books
200 Old Tappan Road
Old Tappan, New Jersey 07675
In U.S. include $1 postage and handling for 1st book, 25¢ each additional book.
Outside U.S. $2 and 50¢ respectively.

Enclosed is my check or money order for $_____

NAME_____

ADDRESS_____

CITY_____STATE_____ZIP_____